colourful gardening

climbers

colourful gardening

climbers

Richard Ross

with photography by **Jerry Harpur** and **Marcus Harpur**

RYLAND
PETERS
& SMALL

Senior designer	Ashley Western
Senior editor	Annabel Morgan
Editors	Polly Boyd, Samantha Gray
Picture research	Mel Watson, Kate Brunt
Production controller	Patricia Harrington
Publishing director	Anne Ryland

First published in Great Britain in 1999

by Ryland Peters & Small

Cavendish House

51–55 Mortimer Street

London W1N 7TD

ISBN 1 900518 80 5

A catalogue record for this book is available

from the British Library.

Printed and bound in China by Toppan Printing Co.

10 9 8 7 6 5 4 3 2 1

contents

Introduction   **6**

Scented   **10**
Clematis   12
Wisterias   14
Honeysuckles   16
Roses   18
Sweet peas, other scented climbers   20
Scented gallery   22

Foliage   **26**
Evergreen climbers and shrubs   28
Ivies   30
Climbers for autumn colour   34
Fruiting climbers   36
Foliage gallery   38

Flowers   **40**
Early-flowering clematis   42
Clematis for mid-spring and early-summer colour   43
Summer-flowering clematis   44
Summer roses   46
Summer twisters and twiners   48
Summer blockbusters   52
Summer climbers with exotic appeal   53
Autumn-flowering climbers, autumn-flowering clematis   56
Late-season roses   58
Flowers gallery   60

Tender   **62**
Tender flowering climbers   65
Tender scented climbers   66
Tender fruiting climbers   68
Hardier climbers   69
Tender gallery   70

Care and cultivation   **74**
Index   **78**
Plant index   **78**
Picture credits   **80**

Introduction

Climbing plants are tremendously versatile. They bring a strong vertical element to planting schemes, and add colour and interest without taking up valuable ground space. Alternatively, some are suitable for ground cover. Climbers are invaluable for their ability to disguise unsightly features – for example, an unattractive fence, shed or tree stump – and to soften bleak building materials, such as concrete or new bricks. They also serve to provide privacy, shade and shelter in gardens in exposed or built-up areas. Above all, climbers are highly ornamental. Many are strong in architectural form, while others produce colourful flowers and berries or striking foliage.

How climbers climb

Climbing plants can be loosely divided into five different types: scrambling climbers; twining climbers; tendril climbers; aerial root climbers; and thorny roses.

Scrambling climbers, like some jasmines or bougainvillea, have flexible stems that, in the wild, nose through and grow over other shrubs and trees. They have no means of supporting themselves, so will require tying to a trellis or wire framework if they are not to clamber over other plants.

Twining climbers, such as wisterias, twist their stems around their supports. Some twine clockwise (such as the Japanese *Wisteria floribunda*), some anti-clockwise (like the Chinese *Wisteria sinensis*). All twiners need some type of permanent support, such as a trellis or wire; alternatively, they may be grown through trees and shrubs.

Some climbers climb using tendrils, which shoot out and coil around their support. A tendril may be a modified leaf stalk, as in the case of clematis, or stem, as in passifloras. Some tendril climbers – Virginia creeper (*Parthenocissus quinquefolia*), for example – cling by means of adhesive pads at the tendril tips,

Right: **Bougainvillea × buttiana 'Mrs Butt' will grow readily in the summer garden, creating a splash of intense colour, but in winter the plant needs a cool, frost-free conservatory.**

which 'lock on' to the nearest surface. The latter require no support, except during the early stages, when they will need the help of canes or wires to guide the plant in the right direction, until it is able to establish contact with its intended support.

Also needing no support are the aerial root climbers, such as ivies (*Hedera*). These produce tiny hairs, or aerial roots, along the stem, and have adhesive pads at the tips that 'glue' themselves to supports like tree trunks, branches and boulders. With tropical plants, such as philodendrons, the aerial roots also latch on to neighbouring plants. The fifth and final group includes those roses with thorns, which anchor themselves as they spread.

Supports

Climbers are usually grown against walls or fences, but there are many other more inventive, quirky ways to grow them: send them up brightly painted poles, antique lamp posts and pillars. Look around architectural salvage yards and scrap yards for strange twisted metal spires. Use ropes, lattice frames, pergolas, trees, a pillar of arched loops, willow frames and wigwams (*see page 74*) – the choice is vast. Several companies sell ready-made iron structures for climbers. If they don't have what you are looking for, you could commission a blacksmith to make something to your specification. Deciduous climbers need attractive supports as the supports are on view during winter months.

Above: **A typical garden of about 30 x 12 m (100 x 40 ft) does not mean that you have only 360 sq m (4,000 sq ft). There is also all that space above ground for dozens of first-rate climbers. Here, sweet peas are seen against a background of violet-flowered *Solanum crispum* 'Glasnevin' and roses.**

Right: **The hop, *Humulus lupulus* 'Aureus', mixes well with a scented rose and a honeysuckle, adding light green foliage to the mixed planting. The hop can grow as much as 6 m (20 ft) in a summer, and is ideal for scrambling over fences and trellis – an excellent way to block out the neighbours.**

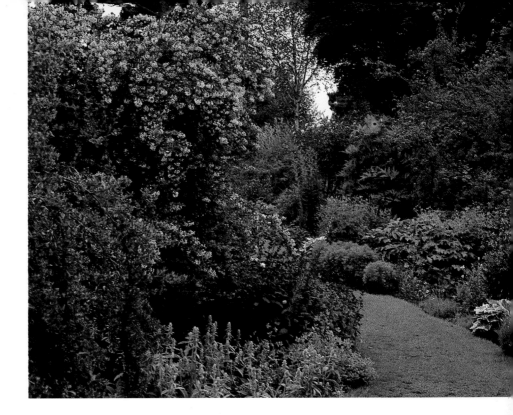

Numerous climbing plants grow happily against the house wall: try vigorous growers like *Hydrangea petiolaris*, which can reach 12 m (40 ft), and *Jasminum officinale*, charging up the drainpipe. Many climbers are suitable for growing in pots in conservatories, such as the tender bougainvillea and the Paraguayan *Solanum rantonnetii*; both may be brought outdoors in the summer.

Growing climbers

There is a host of stunning climbing plants to choose from: some flower prolifically (*Rosa* 'Parkdirektor Riggers'), while others flower for just a few days or have a single burst in summer (*R.* 'Paul's Himalayan Musk'). There are those that provide spectacular autumn leaf colour, such as *Vitis vinifera*, or fragrant blooms, like jasmine.

When selecting climbers, ensure that they are suitable for the site. Some are fairly tender, and require the shelter of a warm wall in cool climates (*Trachelospermum jasminoides*); there are many hardy climbers, however, such as ivies, that survive happily without any protection at all. Many climbers need full sun (*Cobaea scandens*), while several tolerate shade (*Hedera helix*). For year-round cover or privacy, choose evergreen climbers such as ivies.

The weight of the climber, climbing method and rate of growth are also important considerations. Some climbers, such as the *Tropaeolum* species, are slimline whippets, and may be grown against almost any support. However, there are many that are extremely heavy, like *Hydrangea petiolaris*, and these need a strong supporting structure to bear their weight.

You also need to be aware that some climbers can cause damage in certain situations: wisterias can easily climb onto a roof and dislodge loose slates; the adhesive aerial root pads of a thick-stemmed, unpruned ivy can damage cement mortar; and the adhesive tendril tips of Virginia creeper can ruin paintwork. In addition, some climbers are extremely vigorous: *Rosa filipes* 'Kiftsgate', for example, can spread up to 30 m (100 ft).

All gardens benefit from a good selection of ornamental climbers, but in a small garden they are vital. There might be no more room on the ground for plants, but high up there is plenty.

The heights of the climbers that are listed in this book are approximate, as growth will depend on aspect, soil, climate, and the plant's vigour. Fully hardy means plants can survive to −15°C (5°F), frost hardy to −5°C (23°F), half hardy to 0°C (32°F), and frost tender indicates plants that may not survive at temperatures that fall below 5°C (41°F).

Top left: *Hedera helix* **'Green Ripple' is an excellent, all-purpose ivy. A quick sprinter, it grows 2 m (6½ ft) high, putting out large leaves and covering uninteresting walls, fences – you name it. You can even grow it as evergreen ground cover. Like many ivies, it is highly undervalued.**

Above: **The ultimate powerhouse rose,** *Rosa filipes* **'Kiftsgate' can reach as much as 30 m (100 ft).**

Many climbers provide delicious scents that can be enjoyed outside on a balmy summer's evening or inside through an open door or window. Fragrant climbers are best planted in a sheltered, warm site: the more enclosed the space, the more powerful the flowers' perfume will be.

scented

Clematis

One of the earliest of the fragrant climbers is the mid-spring flowering *Clematis armandii* (*Group 1, see page 76*). It has evergreen foliage, bronze when young, and swags of delightful white flowers exuding scents of almond mixed with vanilla. *C. a.* 'Apple Blossom' is also an excellent climber, with white flowers tinged pink. Both need a sheltered, sunny wall where the buds can develop and new growth will not get killed by frost. They can easily grow to 6 m (20 ft), and look good trained along the ridge of a long, low wall, with the scent about face high. If left alone, they will turn into a marvellous, mounding thicket.

The vanilla-scented *Clematis montana* and its cultivars (*Group 1, see page 76*) have plenty of verve and vigour. They flower later, mostly in late spring to early summer, and produce flowers for about four weeks in mauve, pink and white. Many reach 8 m (26 ft) or more, and can shoot up a hedge or tree

Above: *Clematis armandii* is an excellent, unusual clematis. It has long, thin, glossy evergreen leaves, and a gorgeous, rich spring scent.

Right: A rampant *Clematis montana* demands a companion with vigour, like this scented honeysuckle.

Opposite page, left: *Clematis rehderiana* was introduced to Britain by the great plant hunter 'Chinese' Wilson in 1908. The flowers have the soft scent of cowslips.

Opposite page, right: Probably the hardiest montana is *Clematis m.* f. *grandiflora*. It can grow 10.6 m (35 ft) high, and has white flowers set against its dark foliage.

Train *Clematis armandii* along the ridge of a low wall to best appreciate the almond-vanilla scent of its flowers.

(avoid apple trees, which are pink with blossom at the same time). They are also excellent at blotting out eyesores like shiny new sheds or fences; but remember, however, that they are deciduous, so will not offer year-round concealment. *C. m.* 'Mayleen', *C. m.* 'Pink Perfection' and *C. m.* 'Elizabeth' are all pink, the latter having the strongest scent; it also turns whitish in shade. *C. m.* 'Picton's Variety' (deep pink) and *C. m.* 'Broughton Star' (pink) are better for smaller gardens, growing to a more manageable height of 5 m (16 ft).

The pick of the summer clematis begins with the early summer, pale pink *Clematis* 'Fair Rosamond' (*Group 2, see page 76*). It reaches only 2 m (6½ ft) high, but has a delicious whiff of violets. It coincides with or is just followed by *C. montana* var. *wilsonii* (*Group 1, see page 76*), which blooms from mid- to late summer. It grows 8 m (26 ft) high, and some cultivars have a strong scent of hot chocolate. The yellow-flowered *C. rehderiana* (*Group 3, see page 76*), with downturned, bell-like flowers

from mid-summer to mid-autumn, is also a vigorous, swarming climber, reaching 7 m (23 ft). Grow it up a wall or into a tree, so that you can peer up into its nodding flowers.

The final four clematis are all late-summer performers (*Group 3, see page 76*). The most strongly perfumed is *Clematis flammula*, which erupts in a great whoosh of white, almond-scented flowers that stand out beautifully against shiny, dark green leaves. Originally from the southern Mediterranean, it thrives in heat and fast-draining soil. It is excellent sprinting up trees, and can reach 5 m (16 ft) high. Also flowering in late summer is *C.* × *triternata* 'Rubromarginata', with gorgeous red-edged white flowers that smell of hawthorn; at 4 m (13 ft) high, it can easily charge up a fence. The recently reintroduced *C. aethusifolia* is smaller, at 2 m (6½ ft), and produces pale yellow flowers with a lovely scent, reminiscent of cowslips or daphne, in late summer to early autumn. *C. serratifolia*, 3 m (10 ft) high, flowers for about four weeks and smells of lemon.

Wisterias

If you are looking for a big scented performer to clothe large areas in late spring and early summer, consider an oriental wisteria. There are approximately forty to choose from, which basically divide into two groups: *Wisteria sinensis* and *Wisteria floribunda*. Both are twining climbers: the former are Chinese, and coil anti-clockwise; the latter Japanese, and coil clockwise. Wisterias come in a small range of colours, mainly white, pinks, lilacs and blues, and can easily reach 11 m (36 ft).

The Chinese wisteria (*Wisteria sinensis*) and its cultivars are much more vigorous than the Japanese types. The Chinese wisterias flower in late spring and often again in late summer, and have numerous larger, more scented flowers (*W. s.* 'Prolific' certainly lives up to its name). The flowers of *W. sinensis* are lilac, while *W. s.* 'Alba' has glorious white blooms. Avoid Chinese wisterias if your garden suffers from late spring frosts, or they will not produce any flowers.

One of the best Japanese wisterias is the two-toned, blue-violet *Wisteria floribunda* 'Multijuga', which bears the longest racemes, sometimes up to 90 cm (3 ft) long. One was even recorded as having racemes 1.8 m (6 ft) long. *W. f.* 'Alba' is white, and *W. f.* 'Peaches and Cream' is white with pink buds.

Left: **For the best wisteria scent, choose** *Wisteria sinensis*. **In some regions, it can be a gamble, as it flowers in late spring and the buds might get blasted by frost. In good years, however, you can have a superb display.**

Right: **Growing a high-performance wisteria on a wall or pergola means pruning it twice a year, in late summer and winter. If that is daunting, grow the wisteria into a sturdy tree to eliminate the need to prune.**

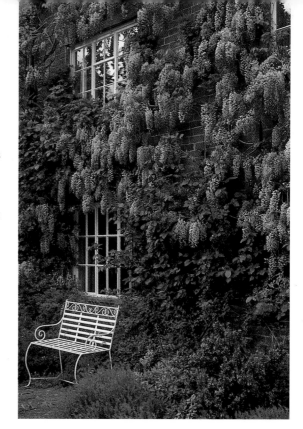

Wisterias create a stunning show in the garden with richly scented flowers and thick, decorative stems.

Opposite page, far left: **The wisteria for long racemes is** *W. floribunda* **'Multijuga'. The flowers are displayed best by training the stems into great looping, twisting shapes. When leafless, they become quite a winter feature.**

Opposite page, left: **Mauve wisterias are very popular, but the white varieties, like this** *Wisteria floribunda* **'Alba', are something else. They give one marvellous flash of white before the flowers fade and vanish.**

Because wisterias have such richly scented flowers – albeit only for about two weeks – and massive stems, they deserve a prominent place in the garden. Grow them as standards, or tie them to pergolas or sunny house walls, sending pruned horizontal branches around windows. Alternatively, train two together to make an arch. Wisterias look good underplanted with tulips and forget-me-nots in spring, followed by alliums with their startling, large round heads, and columbines (*Aquilegia*) in near-black colours. *Wisteria sinensis* looks marvellous growing up a mature yew or hawthorn, with its flowers tumbling out of the host.

Most grafted wisterias – distinguished by the base of the stem being slightly darker than the upper wood – should flower in their third year, provided they experience hot, dry conditions the previous summer and are pruned correctly (*see page 77*). They are unlikely to flower prolifically for another year or two. Chinese wisterias may flower one year earlier than Japanese types. Avoid wisterias grown from seed – they can take twenty years to flower.

Honeysuckles

No garden should be without a scented honeysuckle. The most fragrant is *Lonicera japonica* 'Halliana', which flowers from early summer to autumn. It has a powerful scent, and produces 10 m (33 ft) of thick, tangled growth. It scrambles happily through trees, and also makes an excellent screen, since it is virtually evergreen. To restrict growth and promote flowering, prune it in spring, cutting the old growth back hard at least every other year. The flowers are white fading to yellow, followed by blue-black berries. At its feet, plant the mauve *Nepeta sintenisii* 'Six Hills Giant': this has a large, full habit and reaches about 90 cm (3 ft) high.

Lonicera × *americana* is deciduous and slightly more modest, reaching 6 m (20 ft), with clove-scented yellow flowers and red berries. Tie it to a pillar, pole or obelisk, and grow magenta *Geranium psilostemon* beneath. Alternatively, grow it against a shady wall with the small deciduous fern, *Adiantum pedatum*.

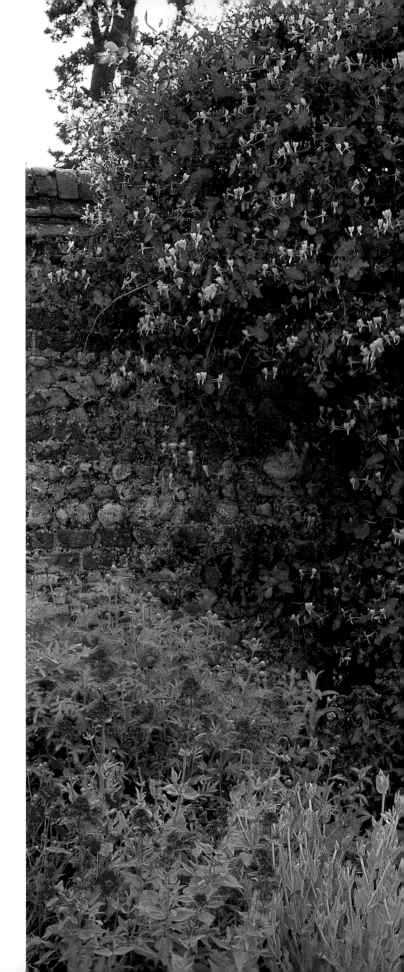

Above: **A structured setting for a display of the scented** *Lonicera japonica* **'Halliana', is provided by the strap-shaped leaves of a phormium and a cordyline.**

Right: *Lonicera periclymenum* **'Belgica' is a superior form of the species hedgerow honeysuckle. It has a strong scent in mid-summer. You could also try** *L. p.* **'Serotina'.**

Roses

Roses are among the most beautiful of all flowering plants and fill the garden with their sweet, voluptuous scents. There is a vast and diverse range for the gardener to choose from, including over sixty climbing and rambling roses.

Climbing roses have large flowers, produced singly or in clusters; most repeat-flower all summer. Climbers are generally slightly more manageable than ramblers: they are ideal for walls and fences (grow them up and around a bedroom window), and can also be trained around pillars, and over pergolas and arches. Climbers often have exposed bare stems near the ground. Prune regularly (see page 77), and use plants such as the purple perennial Stachys byzantina, 45 cm (18 in) high, or blue or white campanula to provide cover around the stems.

There are five excellent red-flowered climbers. Even on light soils, Rosa 'Château de Clos-Vougeot, Climbing' can reach a height of 4 m (13 ft). It has a strong, deep scent, with some later flowers. R. 'Ena Harkness, Climbing' grows slightly taller, at 5 m (16 ft), with hanging heads you can peer up into and some later flowers. R. 'Etoile de Hollande, Climbing' has a fabulous rich scent, reaches 5 m (16 ft), and is recurrent. For a rich, dark purple-red colour, try R. 'Guinée', 5 m (16 ft) high, setting it against a light background for best effect. R. 'Crimson Glory, Climbing', 4 m (13 ft) high, is another excellent climber with large double, extremely fragrant dark red blooms.

Fewer excellent whites are available. There is the impressive whitish pink Rosa 'Madame Alfred Carrière', 5 m (16 ft) high, and the lemon-white R. 'Paul's Lemon Pillar', 5 m (16 ft) high, with a marvellous scent. R. 'Purity', 4 m (13 ft) high, has a strong scent but masses of prickles and few repeat flowers. R. 'Iceberg, Climbing' has a long flowering season, but is only 3 m (10 ft) high. The most vigorous climber is the notorious R. filipes 'Kiftsgate'. It can put on 6 m (20 ft) in a season, and can reach as much as 30 m (100 ft). It needs time to get going, but gives good security and 45 cm (18 in) wide bunches of scented, creamy flowers.

The best scented climbing yellows include the first-rate buff-coloured Rosa 'Gloire de Dijon', 5 m (16 ft) high, with a long flowering season; R. 'Golden Dawn, Climbing', 4 m (13 ft) high, with a delicious scent and sporadic later blooms; and R. 'Lady Hillingdon, Climbing', 5 m (16 ft) high, a richly scented beauty which has a long flowering season and tolerates light, free-draining soil. The 3 m (10 ft) high R. 'Maigold' has a glorious scent and some later flowers. Other good yellow climbers include R. 'Easlea's Golden Rambler', 4 m (13 ft) high; R. 'Lawrence Johnston', 8 m (26 ft) high; and R. 'Leverkusen', 3 m (10 ft) high.

Above left: **The bush Rosa 'Iceberg' may grow only 80 cm (32 in) high, but it sported a climbing version, which was introduced in 1968. R. 'Iceberg, Climbing' grows as much as 3 m (10 ft) high and has glossy leaves with an abundant display of flowers. Extremely reliable, it blooms throughout the summer.**

Above right: **Rosa 'Iceberg, Climbing' can also be grown as a standard rose, pruned to form a white, head-high ball, thick with massed white flowers. Good for livening up the back of the border, it can also be used as a focal point in a more formal, geometric setting.**

Climbing roses are ideal for covering walls and fences — if possible, grow a richly scented type up a house wall and train it around a bedroom window so that fragrance floods in when the window is open in summertime.

Finally, there are some excellent pink climbers. *Rosa* 'Madame Abel Chatenay, Climbing', 5 m (16 ft) high, is exquisite, with plentiful repeat flowers and a rich scent. *R.* 'New Dawn' reaches 1.5 m (5 ft) higher, with glossy foliage and a long flowering season. Just as good are *R.* 'La France', 4 m (13 ft) high, and *R.* 'Madame Grégoire Staechelin', 6 m (20 ft) high.

Ramblers usually have one big burst of small flowers held in large clusters that appear mainly in early summer. They are at their best growing into trees, where their sprays of flowers can cascade over the branches. Alternatively, use any sturdy tall prop like an arch or a pergola, preferably an ornamental one that will still be an attractive feature in winter.

The one-burst ramblers include some vigorous growers. *Rosa* 'Paul's Himalayan Musk', 10 m (30 ft) high, will even put on a decent show in the poor, dry soil under a *Leylandii* and will snake through the host plant, turning it into a sensational wall of delicate pink for a couple of weeks in mid-summer. Another impressive rambler is *R. helenae*, which can hook itself over a 6 m (20 ft) hedge, holding up clusters of scented white flowers.

For a very strong, fruity scent, try the robust white *Rosa* 'Bobbie James', 10 m (30 ft), which looks particularly spectacular shooting into and clambering all over an old apple tree. It has heavier flowers than the otherwise similar *R.* 'Rambling Rector'. Other first-rate ramblers include *R.* 'Albéric Barbier', 6 m (20 ft) high, with creamy white flowers; *R.* 'Albertine', 5 m (16 ft) high, with glorious copper-pink blooms; the creamy pink *R.* 'Félicité Perpétuée', 5 m (16 ft) high; *R.* 'Francis E. Lester', 5 m (16 ft) high, with whitish pink flowers; *R.* 'Goldfinch', 3 m (10 ft) high, in yellow; *R.* 'Paul Transon', 5 m (16 ft) high, in copper-orange; and *R.* 'Seagull', 6 m (20 ft) high, in white.

Above left: *Rosa* **'Rambling Rector' is a robust climbing rose that can reach 7.5 m (25 ft) high. It is traditionally grown into old trees, and with very good reason. It looks absolutely terrific.**

Above right: *Rosa* **'Paul's Lemon Pillar' might be a more modest 4.5 m (15 ft) high, but it has huge flowers in mid-summer. It will do its best when grown against a warm, sunny wall.**

Sweet peas

Sweet peas (*Lathyrus odoratus*) flower from summer to early autumn and are available in a wealth of rich colours, from scarlet to white. They have a pure, sweet fragrance that, on a warm, still day, is detectable even from 6–9 m (20–30 ft) away. Flowers of the recently developed Spencer strain are not as strongly scented as those of the older cultivars. The most fragrant are the purple *Lathyrus odoratus*, 1.8 m (6 ft) high, and the 'Old-fashioned' sweet peas of the same height, in blues, reds, pinks and white, and particularly the wonderful maroon *L. o.* 'Matucana'. Grow sweet peas as annuals from seed, training them up cane wigwams (*see page 74*), or onto horizontal canes, 1.5–1.8 m (5–6 ft) above ground, supported along their length by vertical sticks. Alternatively, grow them up an arch or spreading over topiary. Dead-head sweet peas regularly for extra flowers.

Other scented climbers

The spring novelty is *Schisandra rubriflora*, 6 m (20 ft) high, from India, Burma and China. It is surprisingly rarely grown, even though it is an excellent, vigorous climber, and hardy to -10°C (14°F). Its scarlet, downward-facing, lightly scented cupped flowers are followed in autumn – providing both male and female plants are present – by small red fruits, resembling a string of beads. The deciduous green leaves, 12 cm (5 in) long, turn yellow before they fall. In a slightly milder, more sheltered garden, where temperatures do not fall below –7°C (19°F), try *S. sphenanthera*, which has subtle green and beige flowers. Both *Schisandra* species flower in late spring. Since they originate in forests and woodlands, these plants require a partially shaded site in humus-rich soil in order to thrive. Grow them up horizontal wires fixed to a wall or posts.

Another equally attractive spring-flowering climber is *Akebia quinata*, known as the chocolate vine. It is semi-evergreen, retaining some leaves over winter, and produces lovely small, cupped, chocolate-maroon flowers. It can reach 10 m (30 ft) and needs training up wires to keep it tidy. A single plant produces both male and female flowers with a spicy vanilla scent, but you must hand-pollinate it in spring using a small paintbrush. This climber may also produce sausage-shaped fruits, provided the summer is hot: try growing it against a warm, sunny wall.

If your garden would benefit from a dense evergreen climber with a powerful scent, try *Trachelospermum jasminoides*, which can reach up to 9 m (30 ft) high and produces shiny, dark green foliage and starry, highly scented white flowers from mid- to late summer. It needs a mild, sheltered garden, where winter temperatures do not drop below −5°C (23°F), and fertile, well-drained soil. *T. jasminoides* 'Wilsonii' has bronze foliage that turns a rich red shade during winter. *T. asiaticum* is also frost hardy and about 1.8 m (6 ft) shorter, with smaller, gorgeous yellow flowers.

Jasmines have an exquisite, heady scent that lingers in the air in summer. Choose them carefully, since some are frost tender. The deciduous *Jasminum officinale* is fully hardy, and is ideal for

Opposite page, far left: ***Akebia quinata* is an attractive, unusual climber. Train it up a wall or let it mound over a derelict stump. It has small, eye-catching flowers and reaches 9 m (30 ft) high.**

Opposite page, above left: **The sweet pea is the ultimate scented annual. It looks good trained up wigwams of canes.**

sheltered, warm, sunny walls. It produces white, highly scented flowers, and can easily reach an upstairs window, growing at least 8 m (26 ft) high. *J. polyanthum* also has white perfumed flowers, but is half hardy, so in cool climates needs to be grown in a conservatory (*see page* 72).

With its showy, gently honey-scented flowers, the cup-and-saucer vine (*Cobaea scandens*) is an excellent annual climber. It can grow 4 m (13 ft) in a season, so is ideal for quickly filling gaps. Sow the seeds in mid-spring indoors in pots, and gradually acclimatize the seedlings to life outdoors, before planting them against a warm wall. Nip out the top-growth to encourage plenty of new shoots, and in summer and autumn you will enjoy masses of creamy green fragrant flowers that later turn purple.

Above: ***Trachelospermum jasminoides* has three great virtues – it is evergreen, has glossy leaves, and is sweetly scented throughout the second half of the summer. It requires a warm, sheltered garden to flourish.**

Left: ***Cobaea scandens* is a quick-sprint annual. If there is no supporting wall, let it twine around a shrub.**

Akebia quinata (Chocolate vine)

Height: 10 m (33 ft); leaves: year-round in mild climates; flowers: early or mid-spring; fully hardy but can be susceptible to late frosts

Semi-evergreen, twining climber producing chocolate-purple/maroon flowers with a gentle vanilla scent and sausage-shaped fruits. Requires fertile, well-drained soil in a sunny site. Grow up walls or pergolas.

Pruning: Little required, but in spring remove weak growth, or prune by one-third to restrict the plant's size.

Clematis armandii

Height: 6m (20ft); leaves: year-round; flowers: spring; frost hardy

Evergreen twining climber with vanilla-scented white flowers and copper foliage. Needs a sheltered, sunny site with well-drained soil. Use to clothe a fence or wall-mounted trellis, or to cover an arch, arbour or pergola. Alternatively, clematis can be grown over a shrub or tree.

Pruning: Group 1 (*see page 76*).

Clematis rehderiana

Height: 7 m (23 ft); flowers: mid-summer to late autumn; fully hardy

Deciduous twining climber bearing pale or straw-yellow, downward-facing flowers with a cowslip-like scent. Needs fertile, well-drained soil to thrive.

Pruning: Group 3 (*see page 76*).

Clematis × triternata 'Rubromarginata'

Height: 4 m (13 ft); flowers: late summer and early autumn; fully hardy

Deciduous twining climber with fragrant red-edged white flowers. Needs fertile, well-drained soil to thrive.

Pruning: Group 3 (*see page 76*).

Jasminum officinale (Common jasmine)

Height: 8 m (26 ft) or more in favourable conditions; flowers: summer; frost hardy

Deciduous twining climber producing abundant white, strongly scented flowers. Needs fertile, well-drained soil. Give a high-potash tomato feed in summer, which encourages the plant to flower prolifically. Grows up any garden structure.

Pruning: After flowering, cut back flowered shoots to a strong stem.

Lathyrus odoratus and cultivars (Sweet peas)

Height: 1.8 m (6 ft); flowers: summer to early autumn; fully hardy

Annuals climbing mainly by their leaf tendrils, available in a wide colour range and rich scents, especially the 'Old-fashioned' types. Sow pre-soaked seeds in early spring in pots, using John Innes No. 1. When 7 cm (3 in) high, or when they have two pairs of leaves, pinch out the tops of seedlings; harden off outside, and plant out. Best in humus-rich, fertile soil. They thrive and flower best in full sun.

Lonicera japonica 'Halliana' (Honeysuckle)

Height: 10 m (33 ft); leaves: year-round; flowers: summer to autumn; fully hardy

Evergreen twining climber bearing white, richly scented flowers. Requires humus-rich, free-draining soil in sun or dappled shade. Also needs plenty of water in summer and a thick spring mulch. Grow up walls and trees.

Pruning: Prune mature plants by one-third each spring, or every other spring.

Rosa 'Gloire de Dijon'

Height: 5 m (16 ft); flowers: summer; fully hardy

Deciduous, vigorous climbing rose with buff-yellow flowers. Like most roses, best on fertile, humus-rich, well-drained but moist soil. A good choice for a shady wall. Otherwise, train against a fence, or grow over an arch, arbour or pergola. Can be leggy, so grow shrubs at its base.

Pruning: *see page 76*.

Rosa 'Guinée'

Height: 5 m (16 ft); flowers: summer; fully hardy

Deciduous climbing rose producing very dark purple-red flowers. Train against a wall or fence, or over a garden structure.

Pruning: *see page 76*.

Above left: **Lonicera japonica** 'Halliana'

Above right: **Clematis armandii**

Left: **Akebia quinata**

Below left: **Jasminum officinale**

Right: **Lathyrus** 'Spencer Waved Mixed'

Opposite page: **Rosa** 'Gloire de Dijon'

Rosa 'Paul Transon'

Height: 5 m (16 ft); flowers: summer; fully hardy

Rambling rose with copper-orange buds and slightly pinker flowers, set off by bright, shiny foliage. Like all roses, is best on fertile, humus-rich, well-drained but moist soil.
Pruning: *see page 76.*

Schisandra rubrifolia

Height: 6 m (20 ft); flowers: spring; fully hardy

Deciduous twining climber producing scarlet flowers that are followed by red, bead-like fruits. Thrives in fertile, moist but well-drained soil in sun or light shade. Grow into trees or over a fence or trellis.
Pruning: Thin as required in spring.

Wisteria floribunda 'Multijuga'

Height: 9 m (30 ft) or more in favourable conditions; flowers: early summer; fully hardy

Deciduous twining climber with showy, blue-violet flowers in racemes 90 cm (3 ft) long or more. Requires fertile, well-drained soil, ideally in sun but will tolerate some shade.
Pruning: *see page 77.*

Wisteria sinensis 'Alba'

Height: 9 m (30 ft), or more in favourable conditions; flowers: late spring; fully hardy

Deciduous twining climber with sensational white flowers. Needs fertile, well-drained soil, preferably in a sunny site, but tolerates some shade. Spectacular grown over arches, making long tunnels draped with flowers.
Pruning: *see page 77.*

Far left: *Schisandra rubrifolia*
Left: *Wisteria floribunda 'Multijuga'*

One of the greatest assets of climbers is their ability to act as a screen: they provide privacy and can conceal unattractive structures in the garden. Evergreens are particularly useful for giving cover in winter, while some deciduous climbers have colourful autumn foliage.

foliage

Evergreen climbers and shrubs

The Chilean *Hydrangea serratifolia*, 5 m (16 ft) or more, is one of the best self-clinging evergreens, climbing by aerial roots that 'lock on' to adjacent walls, tree trunks, or any other potential support. Surprisingly – and undeservedly – underrated, it happily grows up shady walls, forming a dense network of branches and leathery leaves, 15 cm (6 in) long, and producing white flowers in late summer. Evergreen hydrangeas are frost hardy, and require a warm, sheltered garden, unlike the deciduous hydrangeas, which tolerate colder weather. Equally underrated is the attractive *Pileostegia viburnoides*, 6 m (20 ft) high. It has beautiful leathery foliage with a big burst of creamy white flowers from the end of summer to early autumn. It also climbs by aerial roots, and thrives in fertile, free-draining soil in sun or light shade. Both *H. serratifolia* and *P. viburnoides* require strong, stout structures to support their weight.

Some *Rubus* species are also terrific climbers, hauling themselves over shrubs and walls, and anchoring themselves in place with their prickles. The 3 m (10 ft) high *Rubus flagelliflorus*, with white flowers and edible black berries, has long, graceful

Above left: **The Chilean climber, *Mutisia ilicifolia*, is slightly tender. However, in cold regions it can be grown as an annual or cut back in autumn and potted up indoors to overwinter.**

Right: **The shiny, evergreen, Chinese *Holboellia coriacea* is definitely worth trying in a warm, sheltered, walled garden. It nearly makes the grade as an essential plant, but can't quite take the full blast of icy, winter spells.**

Evergreen clematis like *Clematis armandii* provide interest in the winter border.

stems bearing large, dark green leaves; tie it to a pergola or tree stump. If you have a large garden, opt for *R. henryi*, which grows twice as high, and has deep glossy foliage. Both are evergreen, and thrive in full sun. Annually, in spring, prune half the stems close to the base – about 30 cm (12 in) above the ground – to force new flowering shoots the following year.

Several clematis are evergreen and will provide interest in the border over the winter; but if you intend to create a screen, bear in mind that clematis will not provide a thick, all-obscuring growth. *Clematis armandii* (*see pages 12, 22 and Group 1, page 76*) is a good evergreen climber, as is *C. cirrhosa* var. *balearica* (*Group 3, see page 76*). Its striking dark green leaves, with glossy undersides, turn bronze in winter, and are accompanied by relatively insignificant yellowish flowers. Grow *C. c.* var. *balearica* in a sheltered, warm site, and provide a support for its 5 m (16 ft) high stems. The new *C. c.* var. *balearica* 'Freckles' has larger white flowers with red markings.

For gardens where temperatures do not fall below –5°C (23°F), try *Holboellia coriacea* or *Mutisia ilicifolia*. *H. coriacea* is a Chinese twiner that grows naturally in shady woodland. It easily reaches 6 m (20 ft), and produces attractive foliage and strongly scented but insignificant spring flowers. Plant it near a strong, stout structure such as a wall, and prune in spring to

Above left: **The shrubby, climbing *Euonymus fortunei* 'Silver Queen' is an excellent shrub that needs occasional judicious pruning to smarten it up and make it shapely.**

Above right: **The evergreen *Clematis cirrhosa* is an early-flowerer. The milder and more sheltered the garden, the more likely this clematis is to flourish. It has yellowish, bell-shaped winter flowers followed by feathery seed heads.**

maintain its shape. *Mutisia ilicifolia*, from South America, is a smaller tendril-climbing evergreen, 3 m (10 ft) high. It produces wonderful pink, daisy-like flowers in summer, and small spiny leaves. Plant it in well-drained soil in a sunny site, with its roots in the shade. Growing it through a shrub is ideal, although walls and strong trellises are also fine. In spring, prune lightly since these plants dislike being severely cut back. The frost-hardy *M. decurrens* is also an evergreen climber of great merit, but is less commonly available.

In addition to the true climbers, there are several shrubs that act as climbers, growing happily up any vertical surfaces. *Euonymus fortunei* and its cultivars are semi-prostrate shrubs for the border, but they will climb up to reach 3–5 m (10–16 ft) if given support, such as a wall. They all thrive in semi-shaded borders, and their shiny green leaves are ideal for brightening up gloomy areas of the garden. The variegated forms include *E. f.* 'Emerald 'n' Gold', which is green and yellow, tinged pink in winter; *E. f.* 'Silver Queen', which is bright yellow in spring, later becoming green and white, turning slightly pink in winter; and *E. f.* 'Harlequin', some of whose leaves can be albino. The leaves of *E. f.* 'Coloratus' turn purple-red in winter. Prune *E. fortunei* and its cultivars after flowering to keep growth in check and to maintain the plant's shape.

Ivies

Often overlooked, ivies make excellent garden plants. There are over three hundred types available: all are evergreen, and they are incredibly versatile and diverse. While some make star performers and are worth growing in their own right, most are ideal as the 'chorus', their foliage providing a luxuriant backdrop to other plantings. They are grown mainly for their leaves, but when they reach the maximum height for their support, they should flower and produce fruit.

There is no need to tie ivies in: just nudge them in the right direction, and they will cling as they go. Unless regularly trimmed, they require a sturdy support , since they can become tangled and heavy. They are fine growing up mature trees, but keep them away from young trees, as well as gutters and window frames. Also bear in mind that they can damage a crumbly wall. Prune as hard as you like in spring, preferably on new growth, to maintain the plant's shape. You can grow ivies in various sites, and on soils ranging from poor to humus-rich, preferably with good drainage.

Ivies vary greatly in vigour: some grow rapidly, others very slowly. They are also available in a wide variety of leaf shapes, both large and small: some are diamond-, fan- or heart-shaped, others resemble bird's feet or have wavy edges. The leaf shape

Opposite page: **Often underrated, ivies have become last-resort climbers whereas some, such as this** *Hedera helix* **'Goldheart', are multitalented. It has the most striking yellow marking of any ivy, keeps its smart looks throughout winter, is the only yellow variegated ivy suitable for shade, and reaches 8 m (26 ft) high.**

This page: **Ivies can be grown up sturdy trees, such as this silver birch, or over a house wall. Do not let them reach the crown of a tree in their weighty adult phase as a top-heavy tree can get blown down. The leaves of ivies are not poisonous, but the seeds should be avoided.**

also depends on the age of the plant: when young, most species usually produce leaves that are lobed, but when they become adult, they tend to produce unlobed leaves.

The colour range and patterning on the leaves of ivies are also highly variable. *Hedera helix* 'Angularis Aurea' is yellow in spring, and chocolate brown in winter; *H. h.* 'Glacier' produces purple-red stems; the leaves of *H. h.* 'Goldheart' have large yellow markings; and those of *H. h.* 'Helvetica' turn red in winter. The all-green-leafed ivies tolerate shade, while the variegated kinds prefer more light.

Hedera helix is a particularly useful ivy, since it will grow and indeed flourish in amazingly poor conditions. Even in a cool, gloomy, damp corner of the garden, it will grow as high as 8 m (26 ft), with masses of shiny green foliage. It is also wonderfully quirky and variable, offering a great diversity of leaf form. *H. h.* subsp. *hibernica* is more like a climbing hedge, making growth about 35 cm (14 in) deep; if you want to keep your garage warm in winter, this is the climber to choose.

Ivy can clothe an unattractive surface quickly, and provides an excellent foil for other plants: reds, yellows and whites stand out particularly well against the green. To cover a large area – such as a wall or fence – choose *Hedera colchica*, which has 25 cm (10 in) long leaves, and a growth span of 10 m (33 ft).

Most ivies are ideal as the 'chorus', their foliage providing a luxuriant backdrop to other plantings.

H. c. 'Dentata Variegata' is useful for walls that lack sun, and generally reaches 5 m (16 ft) high. It has grey-green leaves, 15 cm (6 in) long, with bright creamy yellow margins, and smells of gin when crushed. *H.* subsp. *hibernica* has slightly smaller leaves and grows twice as high, also making it useful for wall cover.

Ivy also doubles as a first-rate hedge filler. *Hedera helix* 'Atropurpurea' livens up a dull hedge with its dark purple winter foliage, as does *H. canariensis* 'Gloire de Marengo', which has gorgeous dark green leaves with silvery flecks and white edging. The latter needs a warm wall in a mild area if it is to be evergreen; in a borderline winter it loses its leaves, although it recovers quickly as soon as spring arrives.

There are numerous other imaginative ways of growing ivy, some of which add a formal or elegant note to the garden. Send them up 3 m (10 ft) high poles at the back of a border, or place them 1.8 m (6 ft) apart, encircling a pond; alternatively, use them to screen an unattractive view. You could also grow ivies over a row of tall, wide arching hoops covered in a strong, tight net, making a tunnel into another part of the garden, or even make an ivy castle using a strong metal frame. Ivies are also useful for growing around statuary, particularly when it is new, since they soften the outline and detract from the brightness of the stone or concrete to provide a sense of timelessness.

Ivies are also excellent for training as topiary shapes. Create a three-dimensional wire frame shaped like a rabbit or penguin – anything with a flowing, rounded outline – then pack it with

Use ivy in imaginative ways to add a formal or elegant note, training it up vertical poles sited at the back of the border, or over a row of tall, arching hoops to form a tunnel into another part of the garden.

moist sphagnum moss and soil-less compost. Plant ivy cuttings 15 cm (6 in) apart, and pinch out the side shoots to make them develop plenty of branchlets. *Hedera helix* 'Ivalace' or *H. h.* 'Miniature Needlepoint' are both ideal for topiary: the smaller the leaf, the more well-defined the design will be. Avoid large-leafed species such as *H. colchica* 'Dentata'.

Opposite page, left: **Never miss a trick with a vertical. Even a dovecote can be upgraded with ivy. You could even erect a series of poles, covered by ivy, to filter a view.**

Opposite page, right: **For detailed topiary shapes, use a medium-, or small-leafed ivy, such as the fast-growing *Hedera helix* 'Ivalace', which has crimped margins.**

Above: *Hedera canariensis* **'Gloire de Marengo' is a fast-growing, variegated ivy. Its foliage provides a good contrast with an autumn-reddening Virginia creeper.**

Climbers often give their most stunning foliage effects in autumn, covering walls, fences and trellis in rich shades of purple, crimson, burnt orange and gold.

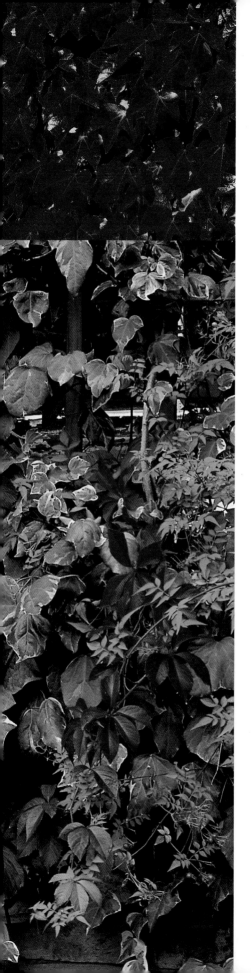

Climbers for autumn colour

Many climbers put on their best show in autumn, with their leaves turning magnificent shades of red, orange, yellow and purple. The degree of brilliance varies from plant to plant, and is determined by a combination of several different factors including autumn light levels, night temperatures, soil fertility, and the length of the preceding winter.

Among the best climbers for autumn colour are the *Parthenocissus* genus, which produce sticky pads at the tips of the tendrils and latch onto fences, trees, or any other available support. Boston Ivy (*Parthenocissus tricuspidata*) is highly vigorous, and can cover a 15 m (50 ft) wall with three-fingered leaves that roar as red as a furnace for three weeks. Virginia creeper (*P. quinquefolia*), with its finely divided five-fingered foliage, is slightly less rampant. Chinese Virginia creeper (*P. henryana*) is a lesser-known, smaller vine, reaching only 6 m (20 ft). Grown for its handsome foliage, it has three- to five- fingered, pointed leaves in soft velvet green, veined white, which turn a fiery shade of red in autumn. All *Parthenocissus* species and cultivars are splendid adorning house walls, but cut them back to avoid damage to roof tiles and guttering. Alternatively, send one up into a large mature tree: its stems will hang down like long red ribbons in autumn. If they get out of hand, cut all *Parthenocissus* vines back in early winter and, if necessary, also in summer.

The *Vitis* genus of vines are frequently grown for their ornamental foliage, often with magnificent autumn colours; some also produce edible grapes. The white *Vitis vinifera* 'Madeleine Angevine' and the black *V.* 'Brant' turn rich plum and bronze-red shades in autumn, and are fully hardy. Most species are fully hardy but some, such as *V.* 'Pirovano 14', require the warmth of a greenhouse in cooler climates. Other first-rate vines for autumn colour include: *V. amurensis*, reaching 12 m (40 ft), with 30 cm (12 in) long leaves; *V. coignetiae*, which can clamber 15 m (50 ft), easily reaching the crown of a tree; the shorter *V. vinifera*, at just 7 m (23 ft) high, and its cultivar that excels in autumn, *V. vinifera* 'Purpurea', with blood-purple foliage. All vines can be reined in if they become too much of a good thing by pruning in mid-winter and again in mid-summer if necessary.

Top left: **Chlorophyll gives leaves their dominant green colour so that, when chlorophyll levels fall at the end of summer, previously obscured pigments – including red, orange, yellow and purple – are revealed. The roaring autumnal red of this *Parthenocissus tricuspidata* is actually the result of dying leaf tissue. This climbing plant can reach 15 m (50 ft), and makes an amazing display.**

Above: **The five-fingered leaves of *Parthenocissus quinquefolia* provide a luxuriant autumn show.**

Left: **This mixed planting features bamboo foliage, *Parthenocissus quinquefolia*, ivy, and the evergreen *Clematis armandii*.**

Fruiting Climbers

Several climbers are grown for their ornamental fruits, some of which are edible, such as the deciduous *Actinidia deliciosa*, which produces kiwi fruit. The fruit is produced in the autumn, and ripens every three years. It is sweet-tasting, provided the summers are hot or the plants are grown under glass; they tolerate cold winters, but can be damaged by frosts in late winter. To produce fruit, both a male and female plant are needed, or a self-fertile cultivar. In the right conditions, *A. deliciosa* can shoot past 10 m (33 ft).

However, the plants may be pruned to 4 m (13 ft), and can be grown in a large conservatory. Note the strict pruning regime (*see page 75*). *A. kolomikta* rarely fruits, but has stunning foliage: the young leaves are bronze, turning pink and white in the sun. Protect the new growth from cats who will revel in chewing the young stems, and it should reach 3 m (10 ft) high.

Above: **The golden foliage of the climbing *Humulus lupulus* 'Aureus', makes a decorative companion for *Rosa gallica* 'Complicata', which has first-rate pink blooms and large leaves.**

Right: **The female flowers, or hops, of the common hop, *Humulus lupulus* 'Aureus', have tiny glands containing chemicals called humulones. These contribute the bitter flavour to beer.**

The deciduous common hop (*Humulus lupulus* 'Aureus') is grown mainly for its brightly coloured foliage and flowers, which are useful in flower arranging; it fruits in autumn. It is a quick sprinter, climbing 3 m (10 ft) in spring, and double that by the end of the season. It is perfect for filling a corner or covering fences and tree stumps. The foliage is golden-yellow and vine-like, and the female flowers, produced in summer, are used for brewing beer.

The final autumn fruiter is *Ampelopsis brevipedunculata*. Its leaves are similar to those of the common hop, and it also grows to 5 m (16 ft), but has masses of blue berries that are particularly noticeable after the leaves have fallen. It requires a sheltered site, preferably against a sunny wall, and wires or a trellis for support. When the sun strikes the berries, their glorious colour looks particularly spectacular.

Below left: **With its blue berries in autumn,** *Ampelopsis brevipedunculata* **outshines the common hop. Do not be tempted by the shorter** *A. b.* **'Elegans' unless you plan to grow it indoors – it will not survive the cold.**

Below right: *Actinidia kolomikta* **needs a long, hot summer to produce fruit. The young bronze foliage turns pink and white in the sun.**

Fruit – edible or purely ornamental – is an additional benefit provided by some climbers, bringing colour to the garden after most plants have finished flowering.

foliage gallery

Actinidia deliciosa (Kiwi fruit)

Height: 10 m (33 ft); flowers: summer; fruit: autumn; frost hardy to fully hardy

Deciduous twining climber grown for its striking, often variegated foliage, flowers and kiwi fruit. Grow up a strong supporting structure like a sheltered, sunny wall, in fertile, free-draining soil. Give a tomato feed during the growing season.

Pruning: Prune in late winter to restrict growth by cutting back side shoots to within three or four buds of the main stem.

Ampelopsis brevipedunculata

Height: 5 m (16 ft); flowers: summer; berries: autumn; fully hardy

Deciduous tendril climber with abundant foliage, producing small green flowers followed by blue berries. Needs fertile, moist but well-drained soil. For a good display of berries, grow on a warm, sunny wall or a robust structure, such as a tree or pergola.

Pruning: Cut back to restrict size in spring. To cover a large surface, prune as for *Vitis coignetiae* (*see below*).

Euonymus fortunei and cultivars

Height: 5 m (16 ft); leaves: year-round; flowers: mid-summer; fruit: autumn to winter; fully hardy

Evergreen scrambling climbers bearing bright foliage with variable leaf colourings. Greenish flowers followed by white fruit. Tolerates poor soil. Grow up walls or trees.

Pruning: Cut back in spring for shape.

Hedera colchica 'Dentata Variegata' (Persian ivy)

Height: 5 m (16 ft); leaves: year-round; flowers: autumn (adult stage only); fruit: winter (adult stage only); fully hardy

Evergreen, clinging by aerial roots, with large, variegated leaves. Prefers fertile, well-drained soil. Ideal for shady walls.

Pruning: Cut back to size in spring. Avoid cutting into four-year-old, or older, wood.

Hedera helix 'Atropurpurea' (Purple-leafed ivy)

Height: 8 m (26 ft); leaves: year-round; flowers: autumn (adult stage only); fruit: winter (adult stage only); fully hardy

Evergreen, self-clinging climber with dark green foliage turning purple in cold weather.

Pruning: *see Hedera colchica* 'Dentata Variegata' (*above*).

Humulus lupulus 'Aureus'

Height: 6 m (20 ft); flowers: mid- to late summer; 'fruit': autumn; fully hardy

Twining perennial with bright yellow foliage and hops (female flowers). Best in sun or dappled shade in humus-rich, well-drained soil. Grow up a strong tripod or over a wall.

Pruning: Cut to the ground in late autumn.

Hydrangea serratifolia

Height: 5 m (16 ft); leaves: year-round; flowers: late summer; frost hardy

Evergreen climber clinging by aerial roots. Produces a good show of leathery leaves and white flowers. Needs a sheltered spot in sun or dappled shade, and a moderately fertile, moist but well-drained, humus-rich soil. Grow up strong, stout supporting structures such as walls.

Pruning: Cut back in spring.

Parthenocissus quinquefolia (Virginia creeper)

Height: up to 15 m (50 ft); leaves: fiery red in autumn; fully hardy

Deciduous tendril climber with orange-red leaves in autumn. Likes sun and shade, and fertile, well-drained soil. Nearly indestructible. Good for large surfaces like walls and trees.

Pruning: Nip back new plants to encourage fresh shoots. Thereafter, prune in early winter and, if necessary, in summer to check growth.

Vitis coignetiae (Vine)

Height: up to 15 m (50 ft); leaves: autumn colour; fruit: autumn; fully hardy

Deciduous tendril climber with bright red foliage and unpalatable black fruits. Thrives in sun or dappled shade, and needs humus-rich, well-drained soil. Grow up strong structures like walls, pergolas and trees.

Pruning: In the first winter, cut back stems by one-third to one-half, and remove the weakest shoots. Thereafter, prune new growth in winter by one-half. When plant fills its allotted space, prune to restrict size.

Top left:
Humulus lupulus 'Aureus'

Top centre:
Actinidia deliciosa

Top right:
Vitis cognetiae

Above:
Parthenocissus quinquefolia

Far left:
Hedera colchica 'Dentata Variegata'

Left:
Ampelopsis brevipedunculata

Opposite page:
Actinidia kolomikta

Every garden, however small, should include some climbing plants. They perform the vital task of clothing featureless walls or other vertical structures, and provide swathes of colour when in bloom. Flowering climbers can interweave with other plants to extend the season of interest.

flowers

Early-flowering clematis

Throughout spring, clematis reign supreme among all the climbers. There are different types of clematis to flower right through the season, providing a colourful backdrop to the emerging spring bulbs. Clematis are often planted singly, with plenty of space around each plant; however, if closely planted, two clematis of similar vigour and contrasting flower colours can look extremely effective whipping around each other. All of the following clematis are deciduous, preferring a warm, sunny, sheltered site, and are in Group 1 (*see page 76*) for pruning. (*See also Scented climbers, pages 12–13.*) The flower forms of different clematis species are very varied, and include nodding bells, open bells, and single, semi-double and double flowers.

 Clematis alpina and its cultivars are excellent climbers and are among the first clematis to come into bloom, flowering from mid- to late spring. They do not exceed 3–4 m (10–13 ft), and look very beautiful when encouraged to scramble over a small tree, shrub, balustrade or low wall. All of the following have beautiful nodding, lantern-like flowers: *C. alpina* and *C. a.* 'Frances Rivis' (with the largest flowers), in a rich mid-blue; *C. a.* 'Columbine', in

a cool light blue; *C. a.* 'Helsingborg', in a bold, clear deep violet; the long-flowering *C. a.* 'Pink Flamingo', in pale pink; and *C. a.* subsp. *sibirica* 'White Moth', in pristine white.

 Flowering slightly later, and prolonging the clematis show of spring-time colour, are *Clematis macropetala* and its cultivars. They also have nodding, bell-like flowers, grow up to 4 m (13 ft) high, and are particularly useful since they are able to withstand shade. The species *C. macropetala* has violet-blue, quite showy flowers, but if you yearn for bold and beautiful colours, its cultivars are even more striking, especially the sugar pink, free-flowering *C.m.* 'Markham's Pink', 3 m (10 ft) high, and the rich mid-blue *C. m.* 'Maidwell Hall', reaching 2 m (6½ ft) high. *C. m.* 'Lagoon' is a vibrant, deep dark blue, and slightly taller. All are first-rate climbers, with extremely decorative, fluffy silver seed heads following on from the flowers.

Opposite page, top right: **Clematis macropetala was introduced to Britain in 1910 from northern China and Siberia. It is hardy, with violet-blue flowers, and seed heads through late summer and autumn.**

Opposite page, below left: **The pale, lavender-blue flowers of 'Maidwell Hall', a cultivar of** Clematis macropetala, **have exotic-looking flowers.**

Left: *Clematis* **'The President' has rich purple flowers, touched with blue. It blooms in three bursts from late spring to early autumn, and reaches 3 m (10 ft) high.**

Right: **The flowers of** Clematis macropetala **are offset by the foliage of the ivy,** Hedera helix **'Buttercup'.**

Below: *Clematis* **'Niobe' has scarlet flowers through summer and early autumn.**

Clematis for mid-spring and early-summer colour

By mid-spring the vigorous species *Clematis montana* and its cultivars begin to bloom. Besides those mentioned on pages 12–13, try *C. m. grandiflora*, with large, 10 cm (4 in) wide white flowers, or *C. m.* 'Tetrarose', in purple-pink. They flower for about four weeks, but are highly prolific and put on a wonderful performance during this time, although some plants might take a few years to get going and flower well.

Clematis chrysocoma has a big burst of faint pink flowers in late spring, and flowers sporadically until autumn. The buds, stems and leaflets have a downy covering. In the wild, it can reach 15 m (50 ft), but in gardens is more likely to reach 5 m (16 ft) or so. It needs excellent drainage, and a protective mulch around the stem to protect against a severe winter chilling. Similar but hardier is the pink *C. × vedrariensis*.

Flowering from late spring to late summer, often with subsequent bursts, are the large-flowered clematis cultivars with single, fully double or semi-double flowers. There are just under one hundred cultivars to choose from. All are deciduous, and fully hardy to frost hardy. All are in Group 2 (*see page 76*). Most reach about 3 m (10 ft) high, and the flowers of the first flush are often 25 cm (10 in) wide. Colours include white (*Clematis* 'Henryi' and the more vigorous *C.* 'Marie Boisselot'); pale pink (*C.* 'Nelly Moser' and the more strongly coloured sugar-pink *C.* 'Bee's Jubilee'); blue verging on lilac (*C.* 'Mrs Cholmondeley', *C.* 'Général Sikorski', *C.* 'Lasurstern' and the vigorous *C.* 'Vyvyan Pennell'); rich violet-blue to purple (*C.* 'Daniel Deronda', *C.* 'Horn of Plenty' and *C.* 'The President'); and bold, vivid red (*C.* 'Niobe').

Late-flowering clematis include vibrant shades of rich pink, red and purple.

Summer-flowering clematis

In summer and early autumn some of the most beautiful of all the clematis come into flower. They tend to flower higher up the stem than other clematis, about 1.2–1. 5m (4–5 ft) above ground, so consider this when planning their role in your garden. They are mostly deciduous and all fall into Group 3 (*see page 76*).

Within the group are numerous large-flowered cultivars, many of them real stunners, all fully hardy and with single flowers. Perhaps the most enduringly popular of all the summer-flowering clematis is the colourful and prolific *Clematis* 'Jackmanii Superba' (also known as *C.* 'Jackmanii'), in a rich, velvety, imperial purple hue; *C.* 'Gipsy Queen' is also deep purple in colour. The bright mauve-pink *C.* 'Comtesse de Bouchaud', 3 m (10 ft) high, is spectacular, as is *C.* 'Ernest Markham', 4 m (13 ft) high, one of the best reds of all the clematis. Another superb red is the slightly smaller *C.* 'Ville de Lyon', which reaches 3 m (10 ft) – ideal for smaller gardens. *C.* 'Victoria' starts off rosy-mauve, then becomes darker, and reaches 3 m (10 ft) high. The blue *C.* 'Perle d'Azur', raised in France over 100 years ago, is taller, at 4 m (13 ft) high.

Clematis viticella and its cultivars produce exquisite, small, bell-shaped flowers from late summer into autumn. The plants need to be cut down to 23 cm (9 in) above ground in spring, so are ideal when positioned to flower above spring- to early summer-performing shrubs, which will cover the stems. They are all fully hardy and resistant to clematis wilt. The species *C. viticella* has elegant, nodding purple flowers, 3.5 cm (1½ in) across, on long stalks, while the cultivars have slightly larger flowers, 5–8 cm (2–3 in) across. *C.* 'Alba Luxurians' is vigorous with pure white flowers; *C.* 'Etoile Violette' is an alluring dark purple; the wonderful *C.* 'Kermesina' has deep wine-red flowers; *C.* 'Madame Julia Correvon' is another rich, deep red; and *C.* 'Royal Velours' is wine-purple. All are 3 m (10 ft) high except *C.* 'Etoile Violette', at 4 m (13 ft) high. *C.* 'Etoile Rose' is another first-rate clematis, producing superb nodding, bell-shaped flowers in rich pink from mid- through to late summer.

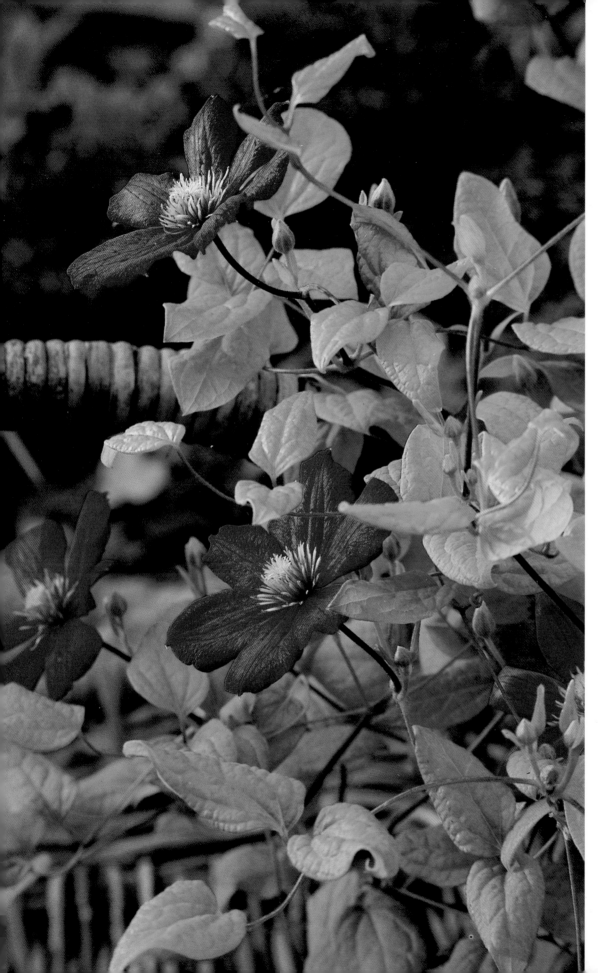

Opposite page:

Top left: **The large-flowering** *Clematis* **'Jackmanii Superba' is an 1878 slightly darker sport of** *Clematis* **'Jackmanii'.**

Top right: **The white-flowered** *Clematis viticella* **'Alba Luxurians' is one of several excellent cultivars from the** *C. viticella* **species, first introduced to England in the 16th century.**

Centre left: *Clematis* **'Comtesse de Bouchaud' is a prolific large-flowered mauve-pink hybrid that blooms generously throughout early and mid-summer. It was introduced in 1900.**

Centre right: *Clematis* **'Kermesina' has gorgeous, rich red flowers. For a smart contrast, grow it through the catkin-like racemes of the evergreen shrub** *Itea ilicifolia*.

Below: **The flowers of** *Clematis* **'Etoile Violette' have bright, contrasting eyes.**

This page: *Clematis* **'Ville de Lyon' should be grown through shrubs because the lower foliage can be unattractive and sometimes drop by mid-summer. The bare stems then need hiding.**

Opposite page: *Rosa* 'Bantry Bay' is perfect for growing up pillars because it is not a prolific sprinter, but instead makes a restrained clump.

Left: **With startling orange-red blooms to brighten a north wall,** *Rosa* **'Danse du Feu' flowers into the autumn.**

There are numerous magnificent climbing and rambling roses that offer great intensity of colour.

Summer roses

Exquisitely beautiful and highly diverse, roses are invaluable in the garden over summer. Besides the strongly scented varieties (*see pages 18–19*), there are numerous magnificent climbing and rambling roses with single to fully double flowers that offer great intensity of colour and variety of form. Several repeat-flower into the autumn. For pruning details, *see page 75.*

Rosa 'Parkdirektor Riggers' gives strong red colour all summer on 4 m (13 ft) high growth. Planted to grow over a pergola, it creates a vibrant walkway or bower. Other colourful climbers, all about 3 m (10 ft) high, include the pink *R.* 'Bantry Bay', *R.* 'Danse du Feu', in orange scarlet, with dozens of sprays of medium-size flowers, and the buff-yellow *R.* 'Penny Rose'.

Large structures and eyesores need more rampant, swamping growth. The gothic arbour in the centre of the white garden at Sissinghurst, Kent, England, is covered by a stupendous *Rosa mulliganii*. It is extremely vigorous, growing 8 m (26 ft) high, and is covered with a mass of small white flowers. The yellow *R.* 'Mermaid' can also cover 8 m (26 ft), but is not as hardy. It needs a warm, sheltered site, and is evergreen in mild winters.

For growing through trees, choose vigorous roses such as *Rosa* 'Belvedere', which can reach 12 m (40 ft) high, with large panicles of pink flowers, and the equally delightful shorter pink *R.* 'Mme Butterfly, Climbing', at 6 m (20 ft). Many buildings are very much enhanced by roses growing up their walls to provide flower colour and sweet, welcoming fragrance. For example, *R.* 'Alister Stella Gray' produces yellow flowers that combine well with those of the wonderful *R.* 'Rose-Marie Viaud', which opens bright cerise and fades to gentle lilac. Both are 5 m (16 ft) high.

Above: **R. 'Parkdirektor Riggers' is the rose with almost everything. It pumps out bright red flowers all summer, has glossy foliage, and is just right for a pergola. Any faults? It has no scent, and is prone to the occasional attack of black spot.**

Far left: *Ipomoea purpurea* is an excellent, purple-flowering annual climber. It is a weed in the tropics and sub-tropics. *I. batatas* is the sweet potato, while the seeds of *I. tricolor* were used as a hallucinogen by the Aztecs.

Left: *Solanum jasminoides* 'Album' scrambles up walls, producing longer-lasting flowers than the species. Its delicate white blooms mix well with *Ipomoea purpurea*.

Summer twisters and twiners

The big summer display comes from roses and clematis, but there are numerous other highly versatile summer climbers. Any of the following may be encouraged to twine around canes and poles, whip through shrubs and tall vertical plants, or cover walls. Bear in mind that they do not need a whole wall to themselves; indeed, several climbers grown together can offer pleasing combinations of colour and form.

Solanum is a vast genus, consisting of about 1,400 species, several of which are climbers. Among the best are the pale blue, summer- and autumn-flowering South American *Solanum jasminoides*, or its stylish white forms, *S. j.* 'Album' and *S. j.* 'Album Variegatum'. They all grow to approximately 5 m (16 ft) high, prefer a warm, sunny site, and are half hardy, although you can grow them as annuals in colder climates. As a precaution, take summer cuttings, keeping them indoors over winter, and planting them out next spring. Alternatively, give the plant a protective winter mulch. Provided it has survived the winter, *S. j.* 'Album' will flower as early as late spring.

Solanum jasminoides and its cultivars are useful in the garden for combining with other plants to flesh out a border scheme: grow them against a wall with purple clematis, flowing into the border to twine around the purple perennial *Verbena bonariensis*, 2 m (6½ ft) high, or the spires of the purple *Malva sylvestris* subsp. *mauritanica*, or an arching *Buddleja*. They are also excellent for larger, more dramatic displays: plant them to weave around a tall standard fuchsia, surrounded by bright yellow *Lilium* 'Citronella' above the spearlike leaves of a cordyline. Alternatively, tie them to a pergola or door frame.

Try also the frost-hardy violet *Solanum crispum* 'Glasnevin', 6 m (20 ft) high, which has a slightly longer flowering period than *S. jasminoides*, and thrives in chalky soil. It is not necessary to tie it to a wall; instead, leave it to form a great twirling mound in the border. The remaining *Solanum* species are frost tender, so keep them under glass over winter in cold climates, or take cuttings. *S. rantonnetii* is purple and grows 1.5 m (5 ft) high; *S. wendlandii* is a pretty lilac blue and the same height; while *S. seaforthianum* has blue, purple, pink or white flowers and grows four times as high. These plants may be placed informally around the garden.

Common morning glory (*Ipomoea purpurea*) is a fabulous, not-too-rampant, 4 m (13 ft) high twining climber with gorgeous, bright purple flowers. It has many excellent cultivars, including the

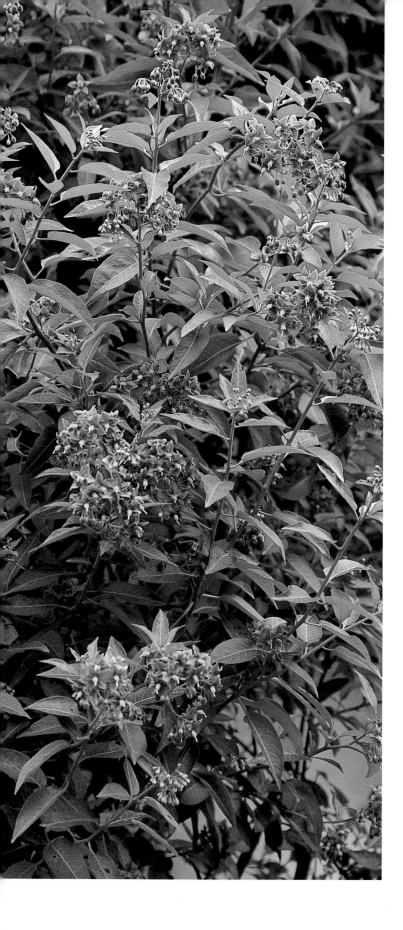

blue *I.p.* 'Dickensonii' and the magenta *I. p.* 'Kermesiana'.
They need a warm, sheltered position, and fertile soil. Train them
around tall lollipop shapes beside a path; alternatively, grow
them in pots to climb above other summer pot plants like the
impressive carmine *Geranium maderense*, with its 60 cm
(24 in) long dissected leaves, begonias, or *Solenostemon* 'Royal
Scot', with its bold, flashy leaves in dark red with apricot patches
and gold margins. The azure *I. tricolor* 'Heavenly Blue' is another
excellent, richly coloured climber. To grow ipomoea from seed,
sow in the spring and pinch out the growing tips of young plants
to produce more growth.

For late-season colour, try the exquisite star-shaped, pale
blue South American *Tweedia caerulea*, which twines 2 m
(6½ ft) high. It also makes good cut flowers. *T. caerulea* is frost
tender and requires fertile, well-drained soil. Sow seed in spring.
The twining tropical African black-eyed Susan (*Thunbergia
alata*), also frost tender, grows about 3 m (10 ft) from spring
seed. Its yellow or orange flowers with black centres climb over
shrubs and up through other climbers. In cool climates it is always
best to grow pots of these colourful annuals under glass, then
bring them out in early summer, positioning them all around the
garden to add vibrant spots of colour.

Violet twining snapdragons (*Maurandella antirrhiniflora*)
are marvellous climbers that need canes or a trellis to whip
through. They grow 90cm–2 m (3–6½ ft) high, with rich violet
flowers outside, white inside, from summer to autumn.
Maurandya barclayana grows about 1.2 m (4 ft) taller in white,
pink or purple, and *Lophospermum erubescens*, 3 m (10 ft)
high, is rose-pink with trumpet-shaped flowers. All are bright,
lively climbers for training through gaps in a hot, sunny site.

Among the greatest of the twisters and twiners are the
members of the *Tropaeolum* genus, which excel at scrambling
through and over hedges, where they run along the surface,
disappear from sight, then emerge further along. They flower
in vivid reds, oranges and yellows, in summer to autumn, and
some are perennials, with underground storage organs.

Left: **Solanum crispum 'Glasnevin' has shrubby growth, making
it an efficient gap-filler in the border. It is the hardiest of the
solanums, but take cuttings in case the winter is severe.**

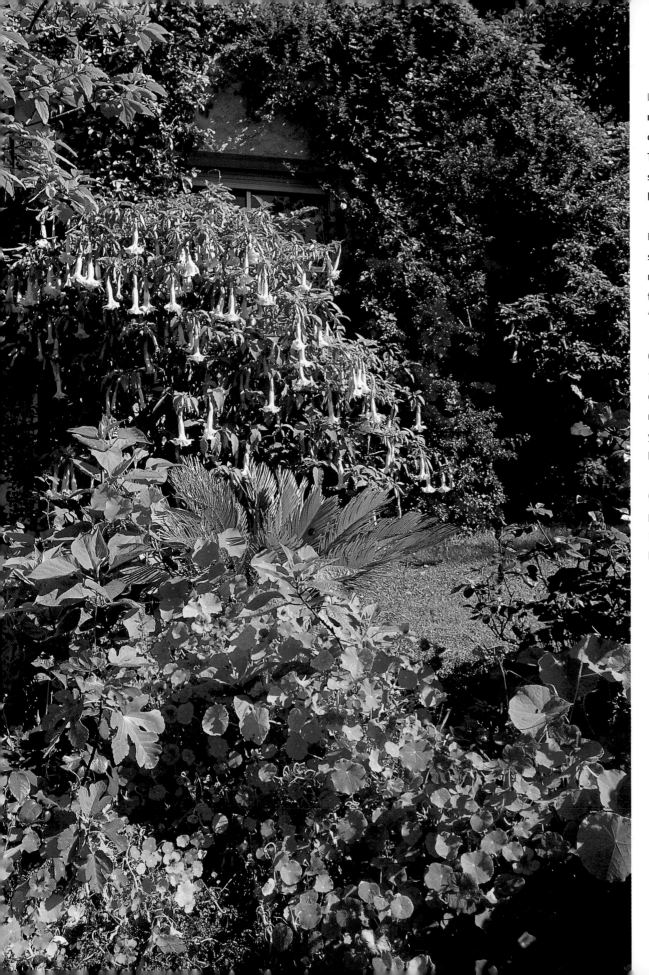

Left: **Orange and yellow nasturtiums give hot splashes of colour in the foreground. They are backed by a soothing white planting and large, floppy-leaved daturas.**

Below: **If there is insufficient space for a tall, run-about member of the** *Tropaeolum*, **family, try the dwarf annual, 'Empress of India'.**

Opposite page, above: *Tropaeolum speciosum* **dislikes hot, dry gardens. Cool, moist conditions are vital if you are to get scores of bright red flowers.**

Opposite page, below: **The ever-popular, tropical African** *Thunbergia alata* **is better known as black-eyed Susan.**

The rhizomatous *Tropaeolum speciosum* grows 3 m (10 ft) high, producing scarlet flowers followed by bright blue berries. It needs a cool, moist garden. Where severe frosts occur, dig up the rhizomes, taking care not to damage them, and store them in a dry, cool but frost-free place over winter. *T. ciliatum* demands similar conditions, but is slightly shorter with old-gold flowers veined red at the centre; one added bonus is that it is evergreen in mild winters. The big favourite, the orange, free-flowering, sun-loving *T. tuberosum* var. *lineamaculatum* 'Ken Aslet' is more tender than those mentioned above, so where temperatures fall below 0°C (32°F) bring it indoors to overwinter, or in mild areas give it a deep protective mulch.

The annual nasturtiums (*Tropaeolum majus*) have the edge over the perennials in terms of popularity and sheer ease of cultivation – simply pop in the large, easy-to handle seeds in sunny spots where they are to grow and remember to water regularly. Visit the garden of the Impressionist painter, Monet, in Giverny, north of Paris, to see them at their most spectacular and be inspired. The approach to Monet's front door, known as the Grande Allée, is a 5 m (16 ft) wide gravelled path. Along the path, at intervals of about 5 m (16 ft), there are tall metal arches covered in glorious climbing roses. Annual nasturtiums line the edges of the sun-drenched path, creeping across it and smothering the walkway in an exuberant riot of green foliage

Use easy-to-grow annual nasturtiums to create a riot of vivid colour.

and vivid red flowers. The same idea may be imitated in any garden, perhaps trailing the nasturtiums around a pond or a plinth, or up and over small hoops in the ground; alternatively, grow them upwards over a 2.5 m (8 ft) high pergola.

Finally, a rare but marvellous scrambling climber is the 3 m (10 ft) high perennial *Caiophora lateritia* from South America. Its five-petalled flowers are the colour of ripe peaches, and are reminiscent of an open rose; they are followed in autumn by spiralling, twisted seed pods. Grow it over shrubs, and provide a thick winter mulch against frosts. The leaves are hairy with stinging bristles, so avoid it if you have children.

Grow vigorous summer-flowering climbers in white or exuberant colours to add interest to vertical surfaces such as walls and trees.

Summer blockbusters

There are two particularly vigorous summer climbers, both of which are deciduous and produce white flowers: the climbing hydrangea (*Hydrangea petiolaris*) and *Schizophragma integrifolium*. Both cling by aerial roots and can easily exceed 12 m (40 ft). *Hydrangea petiolaris* is quite happy on walls that receive little sun, or clambering up a solid, mature tree. It is a big, beefy grower, but takes several years to get going. The flowers last only two to three weeks in the summer, and the dark green leaves turn yellow in the autumn, before falling. Cut plants back in spring.

Schizophragma integrifolium has a longer flowering period of two months, but the flowers can be checked by late spring frosts. Grow it against a wall, with pale green box (*Buxus*) balls in a row at the base, and surrounded by spring tulips and blue agapanthus. A good climber to grow through *S. integrifolium* is the Chilean glory flower (*Eccremocarpus scaber*). It can reach 4 m (13 ft) in a season, and produces bright orange flowers all summer and into autumn. The Anglia Hybrids come in bright, brash colours from pink to orange. In areas with mild winters, this plant can be grown as a perennial. In colder areas, it is best treated as an annual.

Above right: **A well-known 'blockbuster',** *Hydrangea* **petiolaris has a big following. However, its flowers are not as long lasting as those of** *Schizophragma integrifolium.*

Opposite page, above: **The long-flowering** *Schizophragma* **integrifolium has creamy bracts that surround the tiny flowers. The bracts turn pink before fading to beige.**

Summer climbers with exotic appeal

There are numerous summer climbers that are exotic in appearance, yet are easy to grow, even in areas with harsh winters. The South American blue passion flower (*Passiflora caerulea*), with its extraordinary, intricate and elaborate blue and white flowers, is much hardier than it looks: even when its top-growth gets zapped by frosts, new shoots appear the following spring.

Climbers with exotic-looking flowers can be surprisingly easy to grow even in cool areas, although some are best grown in a pot and moved under glass in winter.

It reaches up to 6 m (20 ft) high, and the summer to early-autumn flowers are followed by a crop of exotic bright orange fruits. Two excellent alternatives include the white and pale lilac *P. incarnata* and the white and pink *P. lutea*. Both grow to about 2 m (6½ ft) high and are fully hardy, tolerating temperatures as low as −20°C (−4°F), although the recommended minimum is −8°C (18°F). In warm summers, *P. incarnata* produces edible fruit, more reliably if the plant is grown in a pot and taken inside under glass for the winter months. All passion flowers prefer to be grown on sunny, sheltered walls.

Left: **The flamboyant *Passiflora caerulea* is so striking and quirky that finding the right place for it in the garden can be tricky, as it may not combine well with other climbers. The best solution is to grow it on its own, as here, scrambling through a bench.**

Campsis × *tagliabuana* 'Madame Galen', from south-east North America, is equally exotic-looking and hardy. It is a magnificent climber, with rampant growth, at least 8 m (26 ft) high, with striking orange-red, tubular flowers that are 6–8 cm (2½–3 in) long, and almost as wide. Given warm summers, and a sunny wall, it should thrive. Avoid other trumpet creepers (*Campsis*) unless you live in a very mild area or have a large conservatory, in which case you can grow them in pots.

Spectacular and unusual, the Mexican *Rhodochiton atrosanguineus* is also easy to grow. It can reach 3 m (10 ft), and produces fabulous deep purple, downward-facing, bell-shaped flowers with a protruding vertical, purple-black corolla. The flowers, which keep appearing until the frosts, are followed by rounded capsules full of seeds. Save the seed when ripe, and keep it in a cool, dry place over winter for sowing next year. Train these plants against a warm wall with wires, or an easier option is to grow them in pots with a frame to climb up.

Aristolochia macrophylla is often called the Dutchman's pipe, owing to its wonderfully bizarre, mottled green, curved flowers, thin at one end and bulbous at the other. Its kidney-like, deciduous leaves are 20 cm (8 in) long. It is a frost-hardy vigorous twining climber, reaching 6 m (20 ft), and requires sun and shelter: grow it over a pergola, where its flowers may be best enjoyed. Little pruning is required beyond removing weak or damaged growth in summer, after flowering.

Make the most of a warm, sheltered wall by growing exotic and vibrantly coloured flowering climbers over it to give your garden or patio a tropical look.

Above left: *Aristolochia manshuriensis* can grow 12 m (40 ft) high. It has larger leaves and flowers than *A. macrophylla* and is far superior, but very rare.

Right: From mountainous southern Mexico, *Rhodochiton atrosanguineus* is an easily grown annual with appealing flowers. The stems need support from canes or wires.

Above right and opposite page: In late summer and autumn, *Campsis* × *tagliabuana* 'Madame Galen' produces vivid, orange-red flowers. Grow it on a sunny wall.

Autumn-flowering clematis

Numerous clematis flower into autumn (*all Group 3, see page 76*), many offering fabulous, decorative seed heads as well as single or double flowers in a variety of shapes. For autumn flowers, *Clematis* 'Huldine', 5 m (16 ft) high, is hard to beat, with its white petals with mauve undersides; to get a good view of it, grow it up and over a sunny wall, to enable you to see through the near-translucent blooms. Other excellent autumn-flowerers include the white *C. chinensis*, 4 m (13 ft) high, and the primrose-yellow *C. connata*, 5 m (16 ft) high. *C.* 'Lady Betty Balfour' is a gorgeous purple-blue, reaching 3 m (10 ft) high. *C. flammula* 'Sieboldii' starts off pale white and turns pale green. It is an intriguing climber, slightly resembling a passion flower, but is extremely difficult to grow.

For decorative seed heads, opt for the large, colourful *Clematis* 'Bill MacKenzie', which grows to 6 m (20 ft), and can smother a long stretch of wall or neighbouring plants with its bright yellow flowers and wispy, silky grey seed heads. The less vigorous *C. aethusifolia*, 2 m (6½ ft) high, also produces both yellow flowers and attractive seed heads. In larger gardens, try *C. vitalba*, commonly called old man's beard. It reaches a massive, sprawling 10 m (33 ft), and is covered in white flowers and silver grey seed heads in late autumn and early winter.

Left: **The leaves are coarse, but when the late-flowering** *Clematis* × *jouiniana* **is in full bloom they are obscured by the mass of white flowers. The cultivar C.** × *j.* **'Praecox' is even better and starts flowering about eight weeks earlier.**

Below right: *Clematis* **'Abundance' produces wine-red blooms over a long period from late summer through to autumn.**

Autumn-flowering climbers

The range of climbers that perform right at the end of the season is quite small. However, there are still several good clematis with attractive seed heads, and roses with orange-red or scarlet hips. *Celastrus orbiculatus* in full berry is a gorgeous sight. It has early summer green flowers, followed by pea-size yellow fruit with scarlet seeds inside that last for several weeks. You need either the hermaphrodite form or both male and female plants in order for the plants to produce fruit. *C. orbiculatus* is a vigorous, 12 m (40 ft) grower, and makes a twining tangle that looks sensational combined with an ivy in full berry. Grow it in a cottage garden, where it can zig-zag at will, rather than in a formal planting scheme. The soil must be fertile and free draining for it to thrive.

If you want to use clematis as ground cover, a good choice is the pale blue *Clematis* × *jouiniana*, which, given humus-rich, fertile soil, sprawls across 8 m (26 ft). It looks very effective twining through herbaceous perennials in the border. If you prefer, it can also be tied and trained to a wall. Its cultivar *C.* × *jouiniana* 'Praecox' starts flowering slightly earlier, at the end of summer, but grows to only half the height.

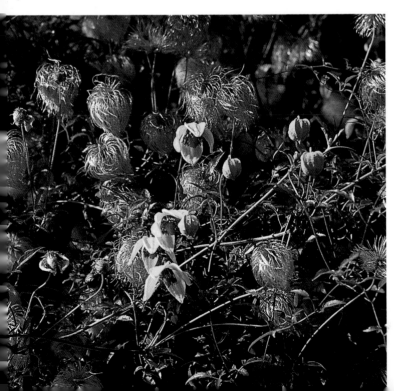

Left: **The large, silvery seed heads of** *Clematis* **'Bill MacKenzie' sparkle in the sunshine. They prolong the season of interest once flowering is over.**

Above: *Clematis* **'Huldine' blooms from late summer to autumn. Stand beneath it to see the light through the flowers. It is one of the best of all the clematis.**

Left: *Rosa* 'Paul's Himalayan Musk' flowers once, in mid-summer, for about three weeks. Until then it gives no hint of the impressive display it will produce. The stems snake up the host – here a silver birch – developing thousands of buds. Then they open, giving a show of blush-pink, followed by small hips.

Opposite page, right: **A first-rate combination is** *Rosa* **'Iceberg, Climbing' growing into a cherry tree. The result is a white display from spring through to the first frosts.**

Opposite page, below left: *Rosa* **'Arthur Bell' is the climbing sport of the award-winning floribunda. It grows 3.5 m (11½ ft) high, flowering into autumn. The yellow blooms age to cream.**

Opposite page, below centre: **The small hips of** *Rosa* **'Francis E. Lester' follow its white flowers and pink buds. The flowers smell like a mixture of bananas and oranges.**

Opposite page, below right: *Rosa* **'Highfield' has pale primrose-yellow flowers to the end of the season.**

Late-season roses

Many climbing roses, unlike the ramblers, repeat-flower from summer into autumn. The yellow *Rosa* 'Arthur Bell, Climbing', pale yellow *R.* 'Highfield', light pink *R.* 'New Dawn', and pink *R.* 'Dream Girl', all 3 m (10 ft) high, are just a few of those climbers that add colour from summer through to the first frosts.

Most roses also provide plenty of brightly coloured berries or hips. Although on display from mid-summer, the hips are particularly welcome in late autumn, when there is less competition from other plants. The best hips are on *Rosa rugosa* and its cultivars, about 1.8–2.5 m (6–8 ft) high, as well as on several wild roses and their hybrids, such as *R. macrophylla* 'Master Hugh', of about the same height.

A selection of small-hipped roses includes *Rosa* 'Bobbie James', *R.* 'Kew Rambler' and *R.* 'Paul's Himalayan Musk', all to 10 m (33 ft), and *R.* 'Francis E. Lester', to 5 m (16 ft). *R. helenae* and *R. polyantha grandiflora*, both reaching 6 m (20 ft), have medium-size hips. For larger hips, choose *R.* 'Allen Chandler', 3 m (10 ft) high, in pink, or *R.* 'Cupid', 5 m (16 ft) high, in peach.

Hips combine beautifully with mauve sweet peas to lift a purple border, and also with the red-purple foliage of *Cotinus coggygria* 'Royal Purple', or the yellow-margined leaves of *Aralia elata* 'Aureovariegata', a form of the Japanese angelica tree. The adventurous can plant vibrant red and orange crocosmias beneath the roses to provide an echoing accent of strong colour around the base.

flowers
gallery

Campsis × tagliabuana 'Madame Galen' (Trumpet creeper)

Height: 8 m (26 ft); flowers: late summer to autumn; fully hardy

Deciduous aerial-root climber with elegant, exotic-looking, slender, trumpet-shaped, orange-red flowers. Requires full sun and fertile, moist but well-drained soil; provide thick spring and autumn mulches. Grow the plant up a wall, fence or tree.

Pruning: In spring, reduce side shoots of young plants by 5 cm (2 in) to form a framework. Thereafter, prune for shape.

Eccremocarpus scaber (Chilean glory flower)

Height: 4 m (13 ft); leaves: year-round; flowers: late spring to autumn; frost hardy

Evergreen, fast-growing tendril climber. Produces showy orange flowers. Requires fertile, well-drained soil in full sun. In cold areas, grow as an annual from seed in late winter at 16°C (61°F). A good climber for scrambling over or through other shrub,s or for growing over a garden structure.

Pruning: Cut back growth in autumn, leaving a small covering as frost protection. Replace with new cuttings every few years in spring.

Hydrangea petiolaris (Climbing hydrangea)

Height: 12 m (40 ft), or more in favourable conditions; flowers: summer; fully hardy

Sturdy, deciduous aerial-root climber with 10 cm (4 in) long leaves with heart-shaped bases and white flowers. Requires fertile, moist but well-drained soil; mulch in spring and summer. Needs a stout structure for support, such as a wall or large, mature tree.

Pruning: Cut back shoots in spring to restrict growth for the available space.

Passiflora caerulea (Blue passion flower)

Height: 6 m (20 ft); leaves: year-round; flowers: summer to autumn; fruits: autumn; frost hardy

Evergreen tendril climber that has spectacular white flowers with blue and purple markings, and yellow fruit. Requires quite fertile, well-drained soil in full sun.

Grow against a wall, or on a pergola.

Pruning: After flowering, prune to maintain shape. Remove feeble growth or frost damage in spring.

Schizophragma integrifolium

Height: 12 m (40 ft); flowers: summer; frost hardy

Deciduous, aerial-root climber with small, slightly scented creamy white flowers, gently fading to pink. The dark green foliage acts as an effective foil to the flowers. Needs humus-rich, moist but well-drained soil to thrive. Can grow in sun or partial shade. Best grown up a strong, preferably sunny, wall or into a mature tree.

Pruning: Little required and dislikes excessive cutting back.

Solanum crispum (Chilean potato tree)

Height: 6 m (20 ft); leaves: year-round in mild winters; flowers: summer; frost hardy

Evergreen or semi-evergreen (may lose its leaves in cold winters). A scrambling climber producing a prolific display of lilac or dark purple-blue flowers followed by cream-coloured fruit. Requires fertile, well-drained soil in full sun to thrive; add a protective spring and summer mulch around the base of the plant. Grow it up around other climbers, or train the shoots on lengths of wire secured at intervals along a wall.

Pruning: Remove weak or dead growth in spring. Cut back unproductive stems to the ground after flowering to force new growth. Wear gloves as the foliage can irritate.

Tropaeolum tuberosum var. lineamaculatum 'Ken Aslet'

Height: 2.5 m (8 ft); flowers: mid-summer to autumn; half hardy

Perennial scrambling climber – the most popular Tropaeolum cultivar – producing vibrant orange flowers over a long season. Requires moist but well-drained soil in a bright place. Water frequently during the growing period. Lift the tubers in autumn and keep them in a dry, frost-free place for replanting the following spring.

Pruning: None required.

Above left: ***Campsis*** × ***tagliabuana*** **'Madame Galen'**

Above right: ***Hydrangea petiolaris***

Left: ***Passiflora caerulea***

Right: ***Passiflora caerulea racemosa***

Below left: ***Solanum crispum*** **'Glasnevin'**

Left: ***Eccremocarpus scaber***

Opposite page: ***Rosa*** **'Arthur Bell'**

Some flowering climbers that will not survive outside all year round can be grown in containers in a conservatory and brought outdoors when the weather warms up. In this way, you can add a Mediterranean feel to your garden in summer with, say, pots of bougainvillea on a sunny patio.

tender

Tender climbers usually benefit from a spell outdoors during the warm months and can make striking seasonal features.

Numerous climbers are frost tender or half hardy, and will not survive outdoors in a frost-prone climate over winter; however, many of the most popular types grow happily in containers in a conservatory. Bring the pots outside into the garden in summer and take them indoors before the first frosts. The plants usually benefit from a spell outdoors, and can make striking seasonal features – for example, imagine potted bougainvilleas in a garden of mirrors and patterned tiles; the large red and yellow flowers of *Gloriosa superba* 'Rothschildiana' growing up canes amongst lettuces; or a scented hoya inside a hot, sunny porch. Below is a selection of tender climbers; there are others, too, not described here, that also require high levels of humidity.

Bougainvilleas are grown for their amazing, brightly coloured, papery bracts surrounding one or three tiny, star-shaped flowers.

Potted climbers will not reach their maximum height, as the pot restricts their root run, but they still need to be kept in check. Most can be pruned lightly in autumn and more heavily in spring. If they become too big, discard them and replace them with a cutting. The heights of the potted climbers given throughout this chapter indicate the maximum size that the plants will reach when grown in a 30 cm (12 in) container.

Tender flowering climbers

Among the most amazing of the tender climbers are the bougainvilleas, which sometimes grow up to 3 m (10 ft) in a pot, but can easily be pruned to restrict their size. Their blooms are not actually flowers, but brightly coloured papery bracts in shades of red, pink, orange and white, which surround one or three tiny, star-shaped true flowers. Be careful when handling bougainvilleas: they climb using quite vicious thorns.

Plumbago auriculata is another tender climber of great merit. The species is available in just one colour, a beautiful, soft pale blue, but there is also a white form (*P. a.* var. *alba*). Both produce generous clusters of slender-tubed flowers and can grow 5 m (16 ft) high, or 1.5 m (5 ft) in a pot, but will withstand hard pruning in spring and winter to keep growth in check. They prefer temperatures of around 7°C (45°F). Water plumbagos plentifully and give a monthly liquid feed during the growing season, and water sparingly in the winter. Several pots of *P. auriculata* look particularly good clustered around a pond.

Few climbers are more dramatic looking than the tuberous *Gloriosa superba* 'Rothschildiana', with its startling, elaborate, bright red and yellow butterfly-like flowers. Despite its exotic, rarified appearance, it is easier to grow than you might think. If you live in a cool climate, plant it up in spring under glass, increase the temperature gradually to 10°C (50°F), then move it outside to a sunny position when the weather becomes warm. As soon as any growth appears, water the plant regularly and give it a liquid feed every two weeks. It grows about 1.8 m (6 ft) high.

Far left: ***Gloriosa superba*** '**Rothschildiana**' **looks too exotic for cool climates, but just needs a kick start in spring in a heated propagator.**

Centre: **Bougainvillea, named after admiral Louis Antoine, Comte de Bougainville, 1729–1811, the first** **Frenchman to cross the Pacific, is so magnificent that it rarely needs companions. However, a morning glory (*Ipomoea*) twining through it looks very effective.**

Left: **The delicate flowers of *Plumbago auriculata* are a lovely pale blue.**

Tender scented climbers

There are many scented climbers, among them *Dregea sinensis*, with its beautiful small, star-shaped white flowers with pink speckling, which reaches 3 m (10 ft) high or 2.2 m (7 ft) in a pot. It can tolerate frost but is best kept at a minimum temperature of 7°C (45°F) over winter. It can survive outside all year in mild gardens, but needs a warm, sheltered position, and a protective mulch. Grow it up a frame of wires, or let it weave over shrubs.

Hoya australis, *H. carnosa* and *H. globulosa* all present their waxy, star-shaped flowers in showy, rounded clusters. *H. australis* has white flowers with a decorative red spot at the base of each petal, and grows about 5 m (16 ft) high. It needs a minimum winter temperature of 10°C (50°F). *H. carnosa* and *H. globulosa* are about the same height, but are slightly hardier, surviving at 5–7°C (41–45°F). *H. carnosa* has pure white flowers, doubles as a trailing plant, and can be grown in a hanging basket, while *H. globulosa* has furry stems. All three need moderate humidity in summer in order to thrive. The best place to grow them apart from a conservatory is in a bright, sunny, well-ventilated porch: place the pots on trays filled with pebbles and water, or mist the growth with a hand spray twice a day. Use John Innes No. 2, with added grit for fast drainage, watering plentifully,

and give a monthly liquid feed during the growing season. Keep the plants cool in winter and do not allow the soil to dry out. Prune either in spring or after flowering to restrict the plant's size, but avoid cutting back hard.

One of the most gloriously scented, and popular, of all flowering climbers is jasmine. The easiest to grow, hardiest jasmine for the garden is *Jasminum officinale* (*see page 21*), but there are also several highly ornamental kinds that require mild winters or the protection of a heated, enclosed porch or conservatory. *J. grandiflorum* has slightly larger flowers – about 4 cm (1¾ in) wide – than *J. officinale* and needs a minimum winter temperature of 7°C (45°F).

Jasminum polyanthum is the indoor pot plant commonly sold in garden centres. Keep its growth in check by pruning and thinning after flowering, possibly reducing old woody stems to within 10 cm (4 in) of the soil. Stand the plant outside in the summer in dappled shade, give it a potash-high feed, never let the soil dry out, and bring it back indoors in the autumn. The Indian *J. sambac* has the largest flowers of all the jasmines, 5 cm (2 in) wide, but is also one of the most tender, preferring a minimum temperature of about 16°C (61°F).

Top left: **For a jasmine with a large flower, grow *Jasminum sambac*. It should keep flowering on and off over winter if brought indoors and kept in a warm room.**

Above: **The scent of the hoya-like *Dregea sinensis* is like fresh honey.**

Right: ***Hoya australis* is named after Thomas Hoy, a 19th-century gardener at Syon House, London. It needs good humidity to thrive.**

Far right: **The scent of *Jasminum polyanthum* is almost overwhelming. Plants do best outside in summer.**

Hoya australis,
H. carnosa and
H. globulosa all
present their waxy,
star-shaped flowers
in showy, rounded

clusters. *H. australis*
has white flowers
with a decorative
red spot at the base
of each petal and
reaches 5 m (16 ft).

Tender fruiting climbers

Some frost-tender *Passiflora* species and cultivars produce sweet, edible fruit. In cold climates, they may be grown inside in pots: overwinter at a minimum temperature of 4°C (39°F) but preferably at about 10°C (50°F). *Passiflora edulis*, which produces the edible passion fruit, has elaborately structured, exotic-looking white, green and purple flowers. The 5 cm (2 in) long fruit continues to ripen through the autumn and into early winter; then it turns purple and eventually drops. Continue watering to keep the soil moist up to this stage, but do not allow the roots to become waterlogged. The chief autumn and winter requirement for *Passiflora* species is bright sunlight. Although the plants are self-pollinating, hand-pollination increases the yield. *Passiflora*

species may also be grown in a heated border in a conservatory. Thread the growing stem out through a small hole in the wall, filling the gaps to prevent any draughts, so that the growth occurs outside but the roots are inside in the warm. *P. vitifolia*, which produces startling, swept-back crimson flowers, 15 cm (6 in)

Top left: **There are scores of excellent passifloras to choose from, and new hybrids keep appearing. *Passiflora vitifolia* has startling red flowers.**

Left: ***Passiflora* × *violacea* has showy flowers from mid-spring to late autumn.**

Above: ***Passiflora edulis* produces sweet edible fruit.**

across, and bronze young foliage, is ideal for this method. Place it near the door so that it receives plenty of fresh air in summer, and provide a heated bed of 7°C (45°F) in winter. In mild weather, it may flower from mid-spring until early winter. It needs pollinating with *P. caerulea*: transfer the pollen with a paintbrush.

Hardier climbers

Some climbers are borderline hardy plants that may survive a mild winter outside if they are given a protective mulch in autumn or winter to insulate their roots. *Dregea sinensis* (*see page 66*) fits into this category, as do two other climbers: the Australian *Billardiera longiflora* and the Chilean *Lapageria rosea*.

Billardiera longiflora, which grows to 3 m (10 ft) in the border or 2 m (6½ ft) in a pot, produces highly ornamental but inedible, fleshy, purple-blue fruits that follow its flowers; its pale green summer flowers are relatively insignificant. It can be grown outside against a sheltered, sunny wall in lime-free soil, provided the winter temperature does not dip much below 0°C (32°F), although 7°C (45°F) is safer. They dislike bright sun; the dappled shade of other shrubs and trees is ideal.

Lapageria rosea, the national flower of Chile, has fabulous, 9 cm (3½ in) long waxy red flowers, on 4 m (12 ft) long stems in a border, or 1.8 m (6 ft) long stems in a pot. It tolerates temperatures as low as −5°C (23°F), although 0–7°C (32–45°F) is a safer minimum, and requires light, cool shade in a moist, lime-free soil, as well as the protection of a wall.

Below: **The Australian *Billardiera longiflora*, the climbing blueberry, forms a mass of growth, 3 m (10 ft) high. The twining, woody stems become covered with purple berries. As with many tender climbers, take cuttings and start again when the plant gets out of hand. This plant is not that fussy and ought to be more widely grown. *B. scandens* grows 1.5 m (5 ft) higher.**

Billardiera longiflora (Climbing blueberry)

Height: 3 m (10 ft) in the border or 2 m (6½ ft) in a pot; leaves: year-round; flowers: summer; fruit: autumn; frost hardy, but prefers a minimum temperature of 7°C (45°F)

Evergreen twining climber grown mainly for its very attractive, globular purple fruits that follow yellow flowers. Keep the roots and pot in shade, and the top-growth out of scorching sunlight. In frost-prone areas, grow under glass in bright, filtered light. In a pot, use ericaceous (lime-free) compost. Water sparingly in winter, and in late winter, pot on or top-dress. If growing outdoors in a mild climate, plants need humus-rich, moist but well-drained, lime-free soil. Keep well watered and give a monthly liquid feed from spring through to autumn. Grow against a house wall, over a pergola or allow to scramble through sturdy shrubs.

Pruning: After flowering, thin out old shoots as required and, if it becomes necessary, trim shoots to restrict the size of the plant to suit the available space.

Bougainvillea cultivars

Height: 2.5–3 m (8–10 ft) in a pot ; leaves: year-round; floral bracts: mainly from summer to autumn; half-hardy to frost tender

Evergreen scrambling climbers grown for the flamboyant colours – rich and pale reds, pinks, oranges and white – of the petal-like bracts that surround their small, tubular flowers. In a pot, use equal quantities of John Innes No. 2 and peat substitute. Plants need a high-nitrogen feed when in growth, and a high-potash feed when in bud; keep the soil just moist when the plants are dormant. Pot on or top-dress pot-grown plants in late winter. Given plenty of light, they may come into flower in a conservatory over winter. In an indoor pot, grow bougainvilleas up a cane frame. Outdoors, they require fertile, well-drained soil. Grow up a pergola, arch or arbour, or against a house wall in full sun. To grow bougainvillea outdoors, choose one of the following tougher specimens: Bougainvillea × buttiana, B. glabra or B. spectablilis. These may survive short cold spells with temperatures down to 0°C (32°F) during the winter months, as long as the soil around them is kept fairly dry.

Pruning: Prune side shoots to within three or four buds of the main stem in early spring; vigorous plants that have outgrown their space may also be trimmed in autumn.

Dregea sinensis

Height: 3 m (10 ft) in the border or 2.2 m (7 ft) in a pot; flowers: summer; frost hardy, but prefers a minimum temperature of 7°C (45°F)

Deciduous twining climber producing highly scented, creamy white flowers up to 1.5 cm (½ in) across, with pale pink insides that are speckled scarlet. The flowers are followed by slim seed pods. To grow in a pot, use John Innes No. 2, with added grit to improve drainage. Water frequently in summer. Outdoors, grow in fertile, well-drained soil, in sun or dappled shade.

Pruning: Cut back the side shoots in spring to restrict the plant's size. It is recommended that you wear gloves to do this, since they leak a very sticky sap.

Gloriosa superba 'Rothschildiana'

Height: about 2 m (6½ ft) in a pot; flowers: summer to autumn; frost tender – withstands a minimum temperature of 8–10°C (46–50°F)

Twining climber producing exotic, elegant, scarlet flowers, with striking yellow colouring on the bases and around their margins. The flowers deepen in colour as they fade. In a pot, plant the tuber 10 cm (4 in) deep in John Innes No. 2, with added grit to improve drainage. In the autumn, reduce watering as the tuber dies back. Overwinter in a cool, frost-free place. Outdoors, grow in fertile, well-drained soil in full sun. It looks most effective when allowed to scramble through other plants, and can be used to extend the season of interest of a spring-flowering shrub whose blooms are over. In frost-prone areas keep the plant in its container so that it can be easily moved back indoors during the winter months.

Pruning: If necessary, cut back shoots to restrict the plant's size.

Far left:
Bougainvillea glabra

Left:
Dregea sinensis

Centre:
Jasminum polyanthum

Below left:
Gloriosa superba 'Rothschildiana'

Below centre:
Lapageria rosea

Below:
Billardiera longiflora

Opposite page:
Jasminum polyanthum

Jasminum polyanthum
(Jasmine)

Height: 3 m (10 ft) or more in the border or 1.2 m (4 ft) in a pot: leaves: year-round; flowers: late winter or early spring in a warm conservatory, or from spring through to summer outdoors in a warm climate; half hardy

Evergreen twining climber with huge sprays of white, highly scented flowers. In a pot, use John Innes No. 2. Water sparingly in winter. Outdoors, plants prefer fertile, well-drained soil in dappled shade or sun.
Pruning: After flowering, reduce the flowering shoots to promote side-growth.

Lapageria rosea
(Chilean bellflower)

Height: 4 m (13 ft) in the border or 1.8 m (6 ft) in a pot; leaves: year-round; flowers: summer to late autumn; half hardy

Evergreen twining climber bearing exotic red flowers. In a pot, needs ericaceous (lime-free) compost with added sharp sand. Outdoors, requires moist but well-drained soil and plenty of leafmould. Needs a cool, partially shaded site in summer.
Pruning: Cut back shoots lightly to restrict the plant's size for the available space.

Passiflora edulis
(Passion fruit)

Height: 4 m (13 ft) in the border or 1.8 m (6 ft) in a pot; leaves: year-round; flowers: summer; fruit: follows flowers in late summer to early autumn; frost tender

Evergreen tendril climber with eye-catching flowers and edible fruit. In a pot, needs John Innes No. 2, with plenty of added grit for drainage. Once buds form, give a tomato feed. Outdoors, grow in fertile, moist but well-drained soil in full sun or partial shade. Dislikes cold, wet soil over winter. Also, beware of over-potting, over-watering and over-feeding, all quite common causes of plants failing to flourish.
Pruning: After flowering, prune shoots to within three buds. Remove any spindly or dead growth as needed. Remove top-growth.

Plumbago auriculata
(Cape leadwort)

Height: 5 m (16 ft) in the border or 1.5 m (5 ft) in a pot; leaves: year-round; flowers: summer to late autumn; half hardy

Evergreen scrambling climber with gorgeous pale blue flowers. In a pot, grow in John Innes No. 3, lightened with sand and peat-substitute. Overwinter at 7°C (45°F). Outdoors, needs fertile, well-drained soil.
Pruning: Hard prune last year's flowering stems in early spring.

Rhodochiton atrosanguineus

Height: 3 m (10 ft); flowers: summer to autumn; frost tender

Deciduous twining climber with black to rosy purple, pendent, bell-shaped flowers. Grow from seed each spring at 16°C (61°F) in light conditions but with some protection from scorching sunlight. Plant in a pot filled with John Innes No. 2 compost, or, when hardened off to outside temperatures, against a sunny wall in moist but well-drained, humus-rich soil. In mild areas, it looks particularly splendid when trained over an arch, arbour or pergola.
Pruning: None required, but pinch out tips to encourage new growth.

Right: **Plumbago auriculata**

care and cultivation

Choosing climbers Avoid plants whose roots are coiled around the root ball or are dangling through the drainage holes.

Planting container climbers against a wall Position the planting hole at least 30–45 cm (12–18 in) away from the wall.

Gently disentangle the roots, spreading them out so that they face away from the wall.

Climbers bring an attractive vertical element to the garden. They can clamber up walls and fences, scramble through other plants, or weave their way around attractive garden structures such as trellis, pillars and pergolas. Because climbing plants make the most of otherwise wasted space, even the smallest plot has room for a climber.

Choosing climbers

Before you choose a climber, first make sure that your garden will be able to accommodate its mature dimensions. If you have a small courtyard, a large climber such as *Hydrangea petiolaris*, with its sturdy trunk, may take over your limited space. However, this does not mean that larger climbers are unsuitable for those with smaller gardens. While some potentially large plants such as wisteria can reach 14 m (46 ft) if left alone, its annual pruning regime, which promotes more flowers, can restrict its height by one-third. Growing a climber in a container, or training it into a weeping standard, also means that its height will be restricted.

It is also important to make sure that the supporting frame will be able to bear the eventual weight and height of the mature climber. Some, such as sweet peas, will be happy with a light wigwam constructed from pea sticks, while others, such as wisteria, require a strong, stout support – a house wall or a sturdy timber pergola.

Climbing plants are usually sold in containers, although some species (such as climbing roses) may be sold as bare-root specimens. Always select a healthy-looking plant with an attractive outline and plenty of healthy leaves and shoots. Bare-root climbers should have sturdy, well-developed, fibrous roots.

Planting and training

Planting against a wall

Since the soil at the foot of a wall can be relatively dry and impoverished, position the planting hole at least 30–45 cm (12–18 in) away from the base of the wall, where the soil will be better and the plant will receive more rain. The hole should be at least twice the diameter of the climber's container.

Hungry climbers such as roses need fertile soil, so prepare the ground before planting by removing any weeds and digging in plenty of well-rotted manure or compost. Plunge the potted root ball in a bucket of water for 15 minutes, until the soil is saturated, then leave it to drain for 30 minutes to one hour.

Invert the pot carefully, supporting the top of the plant, then slide the root ball out of the pot. Plant the climber at the same depth as in its original pot. Clematis are the exception to this rule – they must be planted 6 cm (2½ in) below the soil surface, where potential replacement buds form, ready to grow if the top-growth is damaged, or clematis wilt strikes.

Angle the stem towards the wall at a 45° angle, along a cane if necessary, and disentangle the roots, spreading them towards the garden. Fill in around the plant, then firm down the soil. If planting during a dry spell, water well, especially during the spring and summer months. A spring mulch

8 cm (3 in) deep will help to thwart weeds and prevent moisture evaporation.

Most climbers, except those such as ivy and Virginia creeper, which climb using sticky pads, will need to be tied to a support attached to the wall, or trained onto a frame of horizontal wires. To construct a frame, use strong, galvanized wire. Attach it to vine eyes drilled into the wall, or to battens attached to the wall. Keep the wire 7 cm (2¾ in) away from the surface to ensure good air circulation. The horizontal wires should be about 40 cm (16 in) apart. In the case of a lightweight annual climber, such as *Rhodochiton atrosanguineus*, a ready-made trellis, screwed into battens that have been attached to the wall, is fine.

Trees and shrubs as supports

Climbers adjacent to trees and hedges also need enriched planting holes, and regular watering, but should be planted at least 90 cm (3 ft) away from their host plant, as the two will be competing for food and water. Position a cane between the two plants so that the climber can scramble along to the tree or shrub. Wait until trees are well established before using them as hosts, and plant the climber in the face of the prevailing wind, so that it is blown into its support, not away from it. Grow annual or herbaceous climbers on hedges and shrubs that need autumn or spring clipping, otherwise access to the support for pruning is difficult.

Wigwams and lightweight metal frames

Roses, clematis and lightweight climbing annuals, such as sweet peas, can all be trained up cane wigwams or lightweight obelisks. The enriched planting hole for permanent shrubs can be larger, up to 90 cm square (3 feet square), than for those close to a wall. The tendril climbers, such as clematis, will need initial tying in, but thereafter will clamber happily over the structure. Horticultural string wrapped around the support will give the climber an added leg-up. Training the climber around its support, in flattish, near-horizontal layers, will promote plenty of flowering vertical side shoots. Most climbers, particularly clematis, prefer their roots in the shade and their top-growth in the sun.

Ornamental structures

Heavy, rampant growth requires the strong support of sturdy wooden or metal structures such as arbours, gazebos, pergolas and arches. Attach wires for tying in. Train growth up each support (and along any horizontals), then across the roof. By spiralling growth around supports, many more flowering shoots will appear low down, but the growth will take longer to cover the top.

Climbers in pots

Use sturdy terracotta pots that will not be blown over. Always fill the base with polystyrene chips or small stones to facilitate drainage. Since new potting compost quickly loses its nutrients, for a good flower display, feed with a tomato fertilizer once buds appear. In subsequent years, either repot or replace the top layer of soil and add a slow-release fertilizer. Water regularly, especially in hot, dry weather. When the roots poke through the drainage holes, pot up to the next size container. If a climber grows too large for its position, take cuttings and start again, or root-prune by cutting back the root system and the top-growth by about one-third in spring.

Combining climbers

When choosing several climbers for the same structure, it is important to make sure that they require similar growing conditions, that one will not swamp the other, and that there is no danger of two with very different pruning needs becoming entwined. For an impressive eight-month display, try combining spring clematis and wisteria on a long sturdy pergola, followed by early-summer clematis, summer roses and honeysuckle, then late-summer clematis and roses, followed by the rich-purple autumn foliage of *Vitis vinifera* 'Purpurea'.

For a novel display of climbers, try fruit and vegetables (not strictly climbers, but they can be used as such). Apple trees can be trained as cordons to grow over arches and tunnels. You can also create an open sunny tunnel, with latticed wooden sides, for pears, peas, runner beans, tomatoes and trailing marrows.

Pruning

Most climbers require some routine pruning: it encourages healthy growth and a strong framework, enhances the shape, keeps the size in check, and promotes flowering or fruiting. Routine maintenance may involve removing spent flowers (unless berries form), thinning out crowded shoots, removing spindly or damaged stems, and cutting back to restrict size. Of course, any climbers causing potential damage to roofs, twining around drainpipes, blocking gutters and dislodging slates must also be kept under control. Cut them back well before the problem arises.

When and how to prune

The time of year when established climbers are to be pruned depends on their flowering season. Since climbers flowering from spring to mid-summer usually do so on the previous year's growth, prune them immediately after flowering, allowing them enough time to produce new shoots before the winter months.

Climbers that flower later in the year usually do so on new growth. These should be pruned in autumn or in early spring, before new buds appear. The exceptions to the rule are the berrying or fruiting climbers, which perform after flowering: generally, prune these in spring.

Remove all dead or damaged wood, and cut back weak shoots. Climbers that are outgrowing their allotted space should be chopped back to prevent excessive growth. Always prune stems approximately 2–4 mm ($\frac{1}{16}$–$\frac{1}{8}$ in) above a healthy, outward-facing bud, using sharp secateurs to make a clean, slanting cut.

Pruning clematis

Clematis can be divided into three main pruning groups, based on their flowering time and habit: Group 1 encompasses the early-flowering species and cultivars, which flower in winter and early spring on the previous year's stems; Group 2 is made up of early to mid-season, large-flowered cultivars, which flower in late spring and early summer on the previous year's growth; and Group 3 includes the late cultivars and species, which flower on the current year's shoots in summer and early autumn.

Group 1

Many of these vigorous, early-flowering clematis require little, if any, pruning. After flowering, prune the weak and dead stems, and thin out excessively tangled growth to a new bud. (If you remove all the new growth, there will not be any flowers next year.)

Group 2

In late winter or early spring, before the onset of the new season's growth, remove dead and damaged stems, and prune back healthy shoots to a strong pair of leaf buds. These buds will produce the first crop of flowers.

Group 3

In early spring, before the new growth appears, cut back all growth to a new bud just above the base of the previous season's growth, approximately 15–30 cm (6–12 in) above ground level.

Pruning roses

The pruning method of roses depends on the type (*see page 77*). Most require initial pruning when planted in the dormant season, or in the first spring if planted in summer. Generally, prune established plants in autumn or early spring.

One-burst flowerers can be pruned immediately after flowering, unless there is a show of hips. With repeat-flowerers, remove the spent blooms and cut back to the third bud below to encourage new flowers. In autumn, cut back their flowered shoots by two-thirds, and the main stems to restrict size.

Pruning clematis

Group 1 Clematis Prune any weak or dead stems after flowering, and thin out any excessively tangled growth to a new bud. New growth will ripen during late summer and autumn and flowers will appear the following spring.

Examples of Group 1 clematis:

C. armandii 'Apple Blossom'

C. cirrhosa 'Freckles'

C. macropetala 'Markham's Pink'

C. macropetala 'White Swan'

C. montana 'Freda'

C. montana var. *rubens*

Remove any tangled growth as necessary.

Group 2 Clematis Remove any dead, damaged or weak stems from these large-flowered cultivars in late winter or early spring before the new season's growth appears. Cut back all the remaining branches to just above a strong pair of leaf buds.

Examples of Group 2 clematis:

C. 'Bee's Jubilee'

C. 'Daniel Deronda'

C. 'Gillian Blades'

C. 'Henryi'

C. 'Lasurstern'

C. 'The President'

Prune healthy shoots back to new buds.

Group 3 Clematis These late-flowering species and cultivars produce flowers on the current season's growth. In early spring, prune all the previous year's stems to just above a pair of strong buds, approximately 15–30 cm (6–12 in) above soil level.

Examples of Group 3 clematis:

C. 'Ernest Markham'

C. 'Gipsy Queen'

C. 'Jackmanii'

C. 'Perle d'Azur

C. 'Victoria'

C. viticella

Cut back to a strong pair of leaf buds.

Wall climbers

Do not cut back new climbers at planting if they are to be trained against a wall, or they might revert to smaller bush types. You can, however, nip them back to the next strong bud to encourage plenty of side shoots in spring. Prune established plants annually, according to when they flower (see above). Always cut back to a healthy bud. Clip out any old stems and cut back weak stems to a vigorous shoot. Remove any dead or damaged wood. Where the base of the climber is bare, with all the growth much higher up, cut back the old stems to a height of 30 cm (12 in), but not all in one season.

Arch and pergola climbers

For a wide arch, spread out the shoots to try and cover the full width; on a narrower arch, train the growth up and over the structure. Thereafter, prune as for established wall climbers (above). Against pergolas, little pruning is required beyond shortening the flowering shoots in autumn or spring.

Tree climbers

It is not necessary to prune roses growing into trees.

Ramblers

If left unpruned, ramblers can become tangled and choked with excess growth. They should be cut back in late summer, after flowering. For the first two years, side shoots should be trimmed to a vigorous shoot. After the third year, about a third of the oldest flowering shoots must be cut back to the base of the plant. Tangled, choked ramblers needing renovation can be cut right back. They will quickly recover.

Pruning wisteria

Wisteria have a vigorous habit and require a strict pruning regime initially to create an open structure of branches (and to restrict size in the case of *Wisteria sinensis*); once established, they require a twice-yearly pruning session in mid-winter and late summer to promote flowering.

After planting, reduce the main stem to 90 cm (3 ft) above ground level, and remove any side branches. In the first summer, tie in the new side branches or laterals, removing any unwanted ones, to a frame of wires; cut back other shoots to 15–20 cm (6–8 in) to encourage flower-bearing spurs. In the first winter, prune the leading shoot and the lateral or side shoots to two or three buds. This will help strong new branches to form.

In the second summer, pinch out the tip of the leading shoot and cut back thin, spindly side shoots to encourage a bushy habit. In winter, cut back the new lateral growth to two or three buds.

In the third and subsequent years, only routine maintenance pruning is needed. In summer, cut back the lateral growth to within 15 cm (6 in). In winter, prune again to 10 cm (4 in), leaving two or three buds. Check the ties on the main stem each year.

Pests and diseases

Always buy good-quality plants and choose an appropriate soil and site. Avoid planting too closely together, since congested plants encourage diseases, and water and feed correctly to promote healthy growth. A regular pruning regime is vital, and diseased or damaged stems should be removed as soon as they occur. Conservatory-grown climbers need plenty of fresh air.

Pruning wisteria

First year – summer
Train long twining shoots into position. Cut back other shoots to about 15–20 cm (6–8 in).

First year – winter
Cut back the leading shoot and the side shoots to 2 or 3 buds.

Second year – summer
Pinch out the tip of the leading shoot and cut back thin, spindly side shoots.

Second year – winter
Cut back the new lateral growth to 2 or 3 buds.

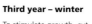

Third year – summer
Cut back the lateral growth to about 15cm (6 in) to encourage flowering spurs.

Third year – winter
To stimulate growth, cut back the flowering spurs to 2 or 3 buds.

Index

Figures in italics refer to captions.

Annual climbers, 20–1, 28, 50–1

Care and cultivation, 74–7
  choosing climbers, 74
  climbers in pots, 75
  combining climbers, 75
  lightweight frames, 74–5
  ornamental structures, 75
  pests and diseases, 77
  planting and training, 74
  pruning, 75–7
  trees and shrubs as supports, 74
  wigwams as supports, 74
Clematis:
  autumn foliage, 35
  care and cultivation, 74–6
  evergreen, 29
  flowering seasons, 42–5, 56–7
  pruning, 75–6
  scented, 12–13, 22–3
Climbers, types of, 6–9

Evergreen climbers, 16, 21, 28–9, 30–3, 60, 61

Flowers, 40–61
  autumn, 56
  early, 42–3
  late-season, 58–9
  mid-spring and early summer, 42–3
  summer, 44–53
Foliage, 26–38, 39
Fruiting climbers, 36–7, 75

Growing climbers, 9
Growing climbers in a conservatory, 63–6, 68, 70

Pruning, 75–7
  clematis, 75–6
  honeysuckle (*Lonicera*), 16
  roses, 75, 77
  Virginia creeper (*Parthenocissus*), 35
  wisteria, 77

Roses:
  late season, 58–9
  pruning, 75, 77
  scented, 18–19, 22, 23–5

Scented climbers, 10–22, 23–5
Supports, 8–9

Tender climbers, 62–9, 70, 71–3
Topiary, 32–3

Year-round cover, 9

Plant index

Figures in italics refer to captions.

Actinidia:
  A. deliciosa, 36, 38, 39
  A. kolomikta, 36–7, 39
Adiantum pedatum, 16
Akebia quinata, 21, 21, 22, 23
Ampelopsis brevipedunculata, 37, 37 38, 39
  A. b. 'Elegans', 37
Aquilegia, 15
Aralia elata 'Aureovariegata', 59
Aristolochia:
  A. macrophylla, 54
  A. manshuriensis, 54

Billardiera:
  B. longiflora, 69–71, 69, 71
  B. scandens, 69

Black-eyed Susan *see Thunbergia*
Bougainvillea, 6, 9, 64-5, 70–1
  B. glabra, 70–1, 71
  B. spectabilis, 70
  B. × *buttiana*, 70
    B. × *b.* 'Mrs Butt', 6
Buddleja, 48
Buxus, 52

Caiphora lateritia, 51
Campanula, 18
Campsis × *tagliabuana* 'Madame Galen', 54–5, 54, 60–1, 61
Celastrus orbiculatus, 56
Chilean glory flower *see Eccremocarpus*
Clematis, 6, 12–13, 22–3, 29, 35, 42–5, 56–7, 74–6
  C. 'Abundance', 56
  C. *aethusifolia*, 13, 56
  C. *alpina*, 42
    C. *a.* 'Columbine', 42
    C. *a.* 'Frances Rivis', 42, 76
    C. *a.* 'Helsingborg', 42
    C. *a.* 'Pink Flamingo', 42
    C. *a.* subsp. *sibirica* 'White Moth', 42
  armandii, 12, 12–13, 22, 23, 29, 35, 35
    C. *a.* 'Apple Blossom', 12, 76
  C. 'Bee's Jubilee', 43, 76
  C. 'Bill MacKenzie', 56–7, 57
  C. *chinensis*, 56
  C. *chrysocoma*, 43
  C. *cirrhosa*, 29
    C. *c.* var. *balearica*, 29
    C. *c.* var. *b.* 'Freckles', 29, 76
  C. 'Comtesse de Bouchaud', 44, 45
  C. *connata*, 56
  C. 'Daniel Deronda', 43, 76
  C. 'Ernest Markham', 44, 76

  C. 'Etoile Rose', 44
  C. 'Etoile Violette', 44, 45
  C. 'Fair Rosamond', 13
  C. *flammula*, 13
    C. *f.* 'Sieboldii', 56
  C. 'Général Sikorski', 43
  C. 'Gillian Blades', 76
  C. 'Gipsy Queen', 44, 76
  C. 'Henryi', 43, 76
  C. 'Horn of Plenty', 43
  C. 'Huldine', 56–7, 57
  C. 'Jackmanii Superba', 44, 45, 76
  C. × *jouiniana*, 56, 56–7
    C. × *j.* 'Praecox', 56–7
  C. 'Kermesina', 44, 45
  C. 'Lady Betty Balfour', 56
  C. 'Lasurstern', 43, 76
  C. *macropetala*, 42, 43
    C. *m.* 'Lagoon', 42
    C. *m.* 'Maidwell Hall', 42, 43
    C. *m.* 'Markham's Pink', 42, 76
    C. *m.* 'White Swan', 76
  C. 'Madame Julia Correvon', 44
  C. 'Marie Boisselot', 43
  C. 'Mme Edouard André', 76
  C. *montana*, 12, 12, 43
    C. *m.* 'Broughton Star', 13
    C. *m.* 'Elizabeth' 13
    C. *m.* f. *grandiflora*, 12
    C. *m.* 'Freda', 76
    C. *m.* *grandiflora*, 43
    C. *m.* 'Tetrarose', 43
    C. *m.* 'Mayleen', 13
    C. *m.* 'Picton's Variety', 13
    C. *m.* 'Pink Perfection', 13
    C. *m.* var. *rubens*, 76
    C. *m.* var. *wilsonii*, 13
  C. 'Mrs Cholmondeley', 43
  C. 'Nelly Moser', 43
  C. 'Niobe', 43, 43
  C. 'Perle d'Azur', 44, 76

  C. 'rehderiana', 12–13, 12, 22
  C. 'Royal Velours', 44, 76
  C. 'Royal Velvet', 76
  C. *serratifolia*, 13
  C. 'The President', 43, 43, 76
  C. × *triternata*, 'Rubromarginata' 13, 22
  C. × *vedrariensis*, 43
  C. 'Victoria', 44, 76
  C. 'Ville de Lyon', 44, 45
  C. *vitalba*, 56
  C. *viticella*, 44, 45, 76
    C. *v.* 'Alba Luxurians', 44, 45
  C. 'Vyvyan Pennell', 43
Cobaea scandens, 9, 21, 21
Cordyline, 16, 48
Cotinus coggygria, 'Royal Purple' 59

Datura, 50
Dregea sinensis, 66, 66, 69–71, 71

Eccremocarpus scaber, 52, 60–1, 61
Euonymus fortunei, 29, 38
  E. f. 'Coloratus', 29
  E. f. 'Emerald 'n' Gold', 29
  E. f. 'Harlequin', 29
  E. f. 'Silver Queen', 29, 29

Geranium:
  G. maderense, 49
  G. psilostemon, 16
Gloriosa superba 'Rothschildiana', 64–5, 65, 70–1, 71

Hedera, 8, 30–1, 74
  H. canariensis 'Gloire de Marengo', 32, 33
  H. colchica, 31
    H. c. 'Dentata', 33
    H. c. 'Dentata Variegata', 32, 38–9

H. helix, 9, 31

   H. h. 'Angularis Aurea', 31

   H. h. 'Atropurpurea', 32, 38

   H. h. 'Buttercup', *43*

   H. h. 'Glacier', 31

   H. h. 'Goldheart', 31, *31*

   H. h. 'Green Ripple', *9*

   H. h. 'Helvetica', 31

   H. h. 'Ivalace', 33, *33*

   H. h. 'Miniature Needlepoint',
     33

   H. h. subsp. *hibernica*, 31–2

Holboellia coriacea, 28, 29

Honeysuckle *see Lonicera*

Hoya:

   H. australis, 66–7, *67*

   H. carnosa, 66–7

   H. globulosa, 66–7

Humulus lupulus 'Aureus', *8*, 36–9,
   36, *39*

Hydrangea

   H. petiolaris, 9, 52, *52*, 60–1,
     61, 74

   H. serratifolia, 28, 38

Ipomoea, *65*

   I. batatas, 48

   I. purpurea, 48, *48*

     I. p. 'Dickensonii', 49

     I. p. 'Kermesiana', 49

   I. tricolor, 48

     I. t. 'Heavenly Blue', 49

Itea ilicifolia, 45

Ivy *see Hedera*

Jasminum

   J. grandiflorum, 66

   J. officinale, 9, 21, 22–3, *23*, 66

   J. polyanthum, 21, 66–7, *67*,
     71–2, *71*

   J. sambac, 66, *66*

Kiwi fruit *see Actinidia deliciosa*

Lapageria rosea, 69, 71–2, *71*

Lathyrus odoratus, *8*, 20–3, *21*, 59, 74

   L. o. 'Matucana', 20

   L. o. 'Spencer Waved Mixed', 21, *23*

Lonicera, 8

   L. × *americana*, 16

   L. japonica 'Halliana', 16, *16*, 22, *23*

   L. periclymenum,

     L. p. 'Belgica', *16*

     L. p. 'Serotina', *16*

Lophospermum erubescens, 49

Malva sylvestris subsp. *mauritanica*, 48

Maurandella:

   M. antirrhiniflora, 49

   M. barclayana, 49

Mutisia:

   M. decurrens, 29

   M. ilicifolia, 28, 28–9

Nasturtium *see Tropaeolum*

Nepeta sintenisii 'Six Hills Giant', 16

Parthenocissus, 6, 9, 74

   P. henryana, 35

   P. quinquefolia, 35, *35*, 38–9, *39*

   P. tricuspidata, 35, *35*

Passiflora, 6, 68

   P. caerulea, 53, *53*, 60–1, 69

   P. edulis, 68, 72

   P. incarnata, 53

   P. lutea, 53

   P. × *violacea*, *61*, 68, *68*

   P. vitifolia, 68, *68*

Philodendron, 8

Phormium, 16

Pileostegia viburnoides, 28

Plumbago auriculata, 65, *65*, 72–3, *73*

   P. a. var. *alba*, 65

Rhodochiton atrosanguineus, 54, *54*,
   72, 74

Rosa:

   R. 'Albéric Barbier', 19

   R. 'Albertine', 19

   R. 'Alister Stella Gray', 47

   R. 'Allen Chandler', 59

   R. 'Arthur Bell, Climbing', 58–9,
     59, 61

   R. 'Bantry Bay', 47, *47*

   R. 'Belvedere', 47

   R. 'Bobbie James' 19, 59

   R. 'Château de Clos–Vougeot,
     Climbing', 18

   R. 'Crimson Glory, Climbing', 18

   R. 'Cupid', 59

   R. 'Danse du Feu', 47, *47*

   R. 'Dream Girl', 59

   R. 'Easlea's Golden Rambler', 18

   R. 'Ena Harkness, Climbing', 18

   R. 'Etoile de Hollande, Climbing',
     18

   R. 'Félicité Perpétuée', 19

   R. filipes 'Kiftsgate', 9, *9*, 18

   R. 'Francis E. Lester', 19, *58*, 58–9

   R. gallica 'Complicata', *36*

   R. 'Gloire de Dijon', 18, 22, *23*

   R. 'Golden Dawn, Climbing', 18

   R. 'Goldfinch', 19

   R. 'Guinée', 18, 22

   R. helenae, 19, 59

   R. 'Highfield', *58*, 58–9

   R. 'Iceberg', *18*

   R. 'Iceberg, Climbing', 18, *18*, *58*,
     58–9

   R. 'Kew Rambler', 59

   R. 'La France', 19

   R. 'Lady Hillingdon, Climbing', 18

   R. 'Lawrence Johnston', 18

   R. 'Leverkusen', 18

   R. macrophylla 'Master Hugh', 59

   R. 'Madame Abel Chatenay,
     Climbing', 19

   R. 'Madame Alfred Carrière', 18

   R. 'Madame Grégoire
     Staechelln', 19

   R. 'Maigold', 18

   R. 'Mermaid', 47

   R. 'Mme Butterfly, Climbing', 47

   R. mulliganii, 47

   R. 'New Dawn', 19, 59

   R. 'Parkdirektor Riggers', 9, 47, *47*

   R. 'Paul Transon', 19, 25

   R. 'Paul's Himalayan Musk', 9, 19,
     58, 58–9

   R. 'Paul's Lemon Pillar', 18, *19*

   R. 'Penny Rose', 47

   R. polyantha grandiflora, 59

   R. 'Purity', 18

   R. 'Rambling Rector', 19, *19*

   R. 'Rose–Marie Viaud', 47

   R. rugosa, 59

   R. 'Seagull', 19

Roses, 8–9, 18–19, 22–3, 24, 36,
   58–9, 74–5

Rubus:

   R. flagelliflorus, 28

   R. henryi, 29

Schisandra:

   S. rubriflora, 20, 24, 25

   S. sphenanthera, 20

Schizophragma integrifolium,
   52, 52–3, 60

Solanum:

   S. crispum, 'Glasnevin', 8, 48–9,
     49, 60–1, *61*

   S. jasminoides, 48

     S. j. 'Album', 48

     S. j. 'Album Variegatum', 48

   S. rantonnetii, 9, 48

   S. seaforthianum, 48

S. wendlandii, 48

Solenostemon 'Royal Scot', 49

Stachys byzantina, 18

Sweet peas *see Lathyrus odoratus*

Thunbergia alata, 49, *50*, 50–1

Trachelospermum:

   T. asiaticum, 21

   T. jasminoides, 9, 21, *21*

     T. j. 'Wilsonii', 21

Tropaeolum, 9, 49, 50

   T. ciliatum, 51

   T. 'Empress of India', *50*

   T. majus, 51

   T. speciosum, *50*, 50–1

   T. tuberosum var. *lineamaculatum*
     'Ken Aslet', 51, 60

Tweedia caerulea, 49

Verbena bonariensis, 48

Vine *see Vitis coignetiae*

Virginia creeper *see*
   Parthenocissus

Vitis:

   V. amurensis, 35

   V. 'Brant', 35

   V. coignetiae, 35, 38–9, *39*

   V. 'Pirovano 14', 35

   V. vinifera, 9, 35

     V. v. 'Madeleine Angevine', 35

     V. v. 'Purpurea', 35, 75

Wisteria, 14–15

   W. floribunda, 6, 14, 77

     W. f. 'Alba', 14–15, *15*

     W. f. 'Macrobotrys', 25, *25*

     W. f. 'Multijuga', 14–15, *15*

     W. f. 'Peaches and Cream', 14

   W. sinensis, 6, *6*, 14–15, 77

     W. s. 'Alba', *14*, 25

     W. s. 'Prolific', 14

Picture credits

The publishers would like to thank the photographers and garden owners for allowing them to reproduce the photographs on the following pages:

Endpapers M. Harpur; 1 J. Harpur; 2 J. Harpur; 3 J. Harpur; 4–5 J. Harpur; 6–7 J. Harpur/Bodiam Nursery, RHS Show; 8 left J. Harpur/design: Tessa King-Farlow, Birmingham; 8 right M. Harpur/Dr & Mrs Stalbow, Stanmore, Middx; 9 left J. Harpur; 9 right: J. Harpur/Kiftsgate Court, Gloucestershire; 10 J. Harpur; 11 M. Harpur/Royal National Rose Society, St. Albans, Herts; 12 left J. Harpur/Springfield Gardens, Spalding, Lincolnshire; 12 right J. Harpur/Rodmarton Manor, Gloucestershire; 13 left Andrew Lawson; 13 right J. Harpur; 14 left Justyn Willsmore/Sir Harold Hillier Gardens and Arboretum; 14 right Justyn Willsmore/Sir Harold Hillier Gardens and Arboretum; 14–15 J. Harpur/ Bradenham Hall, Norfolk; 15 J. Harpur/Home Farm, Balscote, Oxfordshire; 16 M. Harpur; 16–17 M. Harpur/design: Timothy Leese for Mr & Mrs Colin McKay, Norfolk; 18 left J. Harpur/Royal National Rose Society, St. Albans, Herts; 18 right M. Harpur/Royal National Rose Society, St. Albans, Herts; 19 left M. Harpur/ Kypp Cottage, Kent; 19 right J. Harpur/RHS Wisley, Surrey; 19 below J. Harpur/ Royal National Rose Society, St. Albans, Herts; 20 left J. Harpur/ Writtle College, Nr. Chelmsford, Essex; 20 right Andrew Lawson; 21 left J. Harpur/Old Rectory, Sudborough, Northants; 21 right J. Harpur/Secretts, Godalming, Surrey; 22 David Askham/Garden Picture Library; 23 clockwise from top left: J. Harpur/ Kiftsgate Court, Gloucestershire; J. Harpur; M. Harpur; J. Harpur; Andrew Lawson; 24 J. Harpur;

25 Justyn Willsmore/Sir Harold Hillier Gardens and Arboretum; 26 M. Harpur/ Sheila Chapman, Chelmsford, Essex; 27 J. Harpur/ design: Jean Goldberry, London; 28 left M. Harpur; 28 right J. Harpur/Plantsman Nursery, Okehampton, Devon; 28–29 M. Harpur/design: Jorn Langberg, Stanton, Suffolk; 29 right J. Harpur/Helmingham Hall, Suffolk; 30 left J. Harpur; 30–31 J. Harpur/design: Susan Ryley, Victoria, B. C., Canada; 31 left M. Harpur/ Kypp Cottage, Kent; 31 right J. Harpur; 32 left J. Harpur; 32 right J. Harpur; 33 J. Harpur; 34–35 below J. Harpur/design: Simon Fraser, Hampton, Middx; 34–35 top J. Harpur; 35 Andrew Lawson; 36 left: Anne Hyde/Lower Severalls, Somerset; 36–37 J. Harpur/ design: Helen Yemm, Flimwell, Sussex; 37 left J. Harpur; 37 right J. Harpur/Stone House Cottage, Worcestershire; 38 J. Harpur/RHS Wisley, Surrey; 39 clockwise from top left: J. Harpur/Saling Hall, Essex; M. Harpur; M. Harpur; M. Harpur; J. Harpur/ Plantsman Nursery, Okehampton, Devon;J. Harpur/RHS Wisley, Surrey; 40 J. Harpur; 41 M. Harpur; 42 left J. Harpur/Beth Chatto Gardens, Essex; 42 right M. Harpur; 43 left M. Harpur/Royal National Rose Society, St. Albans, Herts; 43 right J. Harpur/ Susan Ryley, Victoria, B. C., Canada; 43 below J. Harpur; 44 top left J. Harpur; 44 top right J. Harpur; 44 centre left J. Harpur; 44 centre right J. Harpur; 44 below J. Harpur; 45 J. Harpur; 46 Clive Nichols/Red Gables, Worcestershire; 47 left J. Harper/Royal National Rose Society, St. Albans, Herts; 47 right J. Harpur/ Royal National Rose Society, St. Albans, Herts; 48 left M. Harpur/Plantsman Nursery, Okehampton, Devon; 48 right J. Harpur; 48–49 J. Harpur; 50 J. Harpur; 50–51 M. Harpur; 51 left M. Harpur; 51 right J. Harpur/

Wollerton Old Hall, Shropshire; 52 top Andrew Lawson; 52–53 Anne Hyde/Mrs Ferguson, Maspin House, Hillam, Yorkshire; 53 Howard Rice/Garden Picture Library; 54 left M. Harpur; 54 right J. Harpur/Parc Bagatelle, Paris; 54 below J. Harpur/design: Dan Hinkley, Seattle, USA; 55 J. Harpur/Villa Roquebrune, nr. Cannes, France; 56 left J. Harpur; 56 right J. Harpur; 57 top J. Harpur; 57 below Andrew Lawson; 58 Sunniva Harte/Garden Picture Library/ Little Hutchings, Etchingham, Sussex; 59 top Mayer/Le Scanff/ Garden Picture Library/Jardin de Talos, France; 59 below left Photos Horticultural; 59 below centre Howard Rice/Garden Picture Library/Royal National Rose Society, St. Albans, Herts; 59 below right David Askham/Garden Picture Library; 60 Anne Hyde/Royal National Rose Society, St. Albans, Herts; 61 clockwise from top left: M. Harpur; J. Harpur; M. Harpur; J. Harpur/Writtle College, nr. Chelmsford, Essex; J. Harpur/ Dr & Mrs Grey-Wilson, Suffolk; M. Harpur; 62 J. Harpur/Philippe Levrat, Hyeres, France; 63 M. Harpur; 64 J. S. Sira/Garden Picture Library; 64–65 J. Harpur/ Philippe Levrat, Hyeres, France; 65 M. Harpur; 66 left Howard Rice/ Garden Picture Library; 66 right John Glover/ Garden Picture Library; 67 left Andrew Lawson; 67 right Andrew Lawson; 68 top left Howard Rice/Garden Picture Library; 68 below left Justyn Willsmore/ RHS Wisley, Surrey; 68 centre right Irene Windridge/A–Z Botanical; 69 Andrew Lawson; 70 Howard Rice/ Garden Picture Library; 71 clockwise from top left: M. Harpur; Howard Rice/ Garden Picture Library; Howard Rice/Garden Picture Library; M. Harpur; Andrew Lawson; J. Harpur/Simone de Chazal, Funchal, Madeira; 72–73 J. Harpur; 80 J. Harpur.